To Audrey

CW01067286

RADIANT FRIENDS BESIDE ME

Very best wishes,

Kevin McGrath

Kevin McGrath

Kevin '98

Krystina Bradley

573641
of 7

First published in Great Britain 1997 by
Krystina Bradley, Beau Centre,
Altrincham, Cheshire,
WA14 1HY

ISBN 0-9531712-0-5

Printed and Typeset in Great Britain
by Bollington Printshop
The Old Stables, Queen Street, Bollington
Macclesfield, Cheshire SK10 5PS

INTRODUCTION

"This book is a compelling account of many unforgettable life experiences, a remarkable spiritual development, and the enthralling but authentic supernatural case histories of Kevin McGrath, a unique Psychic of his time."

H. F. HUTSON

"I have found Kevin McGrath to be a dedicated and highly gifted spiritual servant. He has a truly remarkable story to tell."

JOHN W SHAW M.A. PhD.
Associate Professor
Columbia Pacific University
San Rafael, California
U.S.A

ACKNOWLEDGMENTS

My deep gratitude to be especially extended to Janet, my dear wife, for tolerating such a bizarre partner for the past twenty seven years and for her many hours of work during the preparation and completion of this book.

Many thanks to Grethe Sonnenburg, Frank Hutson, Margaret Owens, Lisa Birchall and Sue Ellis for their thankless invaluable support, and to all those who have kindly shared their psychic experiences.

Thank you also to the SOCIETY OF THE INNER LIGHT, London, and my special thanks to The Psychic News.

DEDICATION

A special dedication to my dad and two deeply loved ladies, my mum and dear wife Janet.

For all my fellow souls, I hope that my spiritual mission unfolded within the pages of this book provides a clearer insight into the complex life tapestry that our universal father continually weaves for the evolution of the spirit.

CHAPTER ONE

My spiritual mission began with a most interesting family tree of continental origin. The varied roots were established through my mother Catherine Soderberg, the daughter of a Swedish national father, and an Irish mother, who was of part Norwegian, French and Irish descent, whose surnames were Buenberg, Laurent, and Cavanagh respectively. Both her parents were of the Roman Catholic faith and lived in Liverpool.

Her father, by all accounts, was a quiet, studious, intelligent man who was initially employed as a ship's carpenter and latterly owned a prosperous tobacco business. My grandmother was employed part-time by relatives working in their hostel which accommodated foreign seamen.

My grandmother also happened to have strong Irish Catholic sympathies. This I gathered from my mother, who remembered her waiting at the roadside for the annual Orange Day Parade and gleefully without warning, hurling the Irish tricolor into the march, causing a near riot.

Sadly, my grandmother died at the age of forty from a brain haemorrhage; my grandfather passing on not too long afterwards with pneumonia. My mother was then housed with relatives in Liverpool and eventually met my father whilst on a visit to Warrington. They were married in Warrington on her 21st birthday.

My parents moved house several times in the early years of their marriage before finally settling into a new council house on Dallam Estate on the outskirts of Warrington, a medium sized town situated between Manchester and Liverpool. Mother, unfortunately, lost her first child Monica, aged two through gastro-enteritis, before my brother Philip was born seven years later.

My father, also christened Philip, was born in Warrington, the son of two Irish parents, both Roman Catholics. Having trained and worked as a rigger in his early years, he subsequently served with the RAF during the second world war. His five campaign medals are presently placed with pride on my hall wall. My father eventually secured regular employment with the local council as a labourer on the highways, and my parents moved into an old dilapidated terraced house near the centre of Warrington, number 13, Elizabeth Street.

The earth entrance for my spiritual task took place with my birth, on the 1st August 1946 at 8.00 am, in Warrington General Hospital. This incarnation was at a time of my choosing with the direction of my soul group and three members of this spirit intelligentsia assigned to be my spiritual guides. The Irish midwife at the time of my birth suggested I should be called Kevin after one of the early Irish saints. This was the beginning of my chosen spiritual and psychic task.

The winter following my birth was very harsh indeed, actually one of the severest recorded this century, not very suitable for myself, a Leo subject who is astrologically ruled by the sun, needing warmth. I feel sure that, as an infant, I would have felt very cold throughout the 1946/47 winter from the beginning of this earth life.

Before I reached my first birthday, I suffered an umbilical hernia, and was rushed to hospital for my first successful operation. At the age of three, it was noticed that I was suffering from severe stomach pains. My mother immediately called in the doctor when I became seriously ill. Peritonitis was immediately diagnosed; I was again rushed into hospital and quickly lapsed into a coma. The priest was brought in and the last rites were administered.

As it happened, on this particular day, there was another boy who had been admitted to the ward with the same condition. The doctor said a new drug had been given to him and, as it had worked positively, he was hopeful that it might work for me, and he would like to try it. I was sinking fast but its usage proved successful and I recovered very quickly. I am now aware that near death experiences, although traumatic, usually open up the psychic senses. This traumatic episode was part of God's plan for my future tasks.

I was five when my sister Angela, the apple of my Father's eye, was born. He had been eagerly awaiting the arrival of a girl since my sister Monica had died previously through illness.

I vividly remember the house on the Dallam Council estate where my parents had finally settled. It was very spartan and cold. There were neither carpets nor wallpaper. In the bedroom where I slept, it was very damp. I was always very chesty as a child, suffering from bouts of chronic bronchitis.

As I was maturing, I felt a great affinity to bees, plants insects, birds, and to cats in particular. I was very wary of dogs. Although I loved them, I kept my distance because when I was six years old, a large black dog, a crossbreed, leapt on me from a nearby garden and bit my leg quite badly. The estate had many such fierce, uncontrolled strays. I never approached them until I knew that they were friendly. I possessed an in-built sensitivity which told me which dogs fell into this category.

As a young boy in my sixth year, I remember walking through the nearby meadows, looking around, inquisitively, and exploring the area by the canal. I remember my father arriving on his bicycle accompanied by our little mongrel dog Rex, a very loyal animal, despite being kept in a shoddy little kennel and never being allowed indoors, which I found unreasonable. After a severe telling off for wandering near the canal my father produced a leather belt with a massive buckle and periodically thrashed me with it, whilst hurrying me on the way home. I remember ducking, to avoid contact, but the blows still bounced painfully off my head. The punishment was an unforgettable experience - I knew that I didn't deserve this kind of treatment.

When I spoke of this incident recently with my mother, she swore that my father never once hurt her physically, and she will insist on dismissing the physical abuse I suffered in the same manner. In reality, the only action required at the time was to take me to one side and explain to me the possible dangers that the local canal presented. I did not need to be physically assaulted, but he could not see it any other way. I felt very angry about this episode and probably felt resentful towards my father for a very long time afterwards.

During my early childhood I recall brief moments of inner satisfaction which the insects and birds provided. I was most happy when a butterfly chose to land on me or especially when a songbird would stay put as I approached it, letting me listen to its beautiful warbling. I also felt a sense of comfort when I was surrounded by large trees whilst walking through the nearby woods. I decided that I owned all the beautiful garden spiders in our rear garden, named them accordingly, and spoke to each one in turn as they settled in their webs.

The following year a pair of brown mice chose the bottom of our yard for residence. I was thrilled on discovering their choice of our house, and for the best part of a week was most excited, constantly lifting the mound and watching the resultant offspring. My joy quickly turned to sadness when I arrived home at the end of the week, to have my mother inform me dispassionately that she had discovered the nest and asked my father to lift the mice out and destroy them. I was heartbroken, and to make matters worse, they could not understand why the destruction of vermin should cause me so much concern. I felt the mice had done no wrong at all, being so cute and harmless; my parents felt otherwise.

Later in the summer a wasps' nest was discovered in the rear garden on the bank of a privet hedge. They happily swarmed in and out of their 'des res' throughout the day. I enjoyed watching them immensely, then ... 'ALARM' - my mother, on finding it, decided to pour bleach down their little home. In a state of panic and to prove they would not harm anyone, I lay head first at the mouth of the nest entrance for a full hour. They poured out during this time in a regular stream, walked on my face and did not sting me once. My mother relented. 'I HAD SAVED THEM!!!' I then thanked the wasps for acceding to my request to be on their best behaviour.

Leo's do not take kindly to being rejected. A very early experience was ingrained on my memory during the annual Walking Day festivities when the local population, children and adults alike, would walk through the town with their church banners. By this time I was eight and this was my first walk dressed up in all my finery, taking part with the Sacred Heart primary school.

The accepted tradition was for relatives and neighbours to run out from the roadside to place money into the children's purses whilst they walked. Every other child in my procession had their purses filled with coins but mine was empty. I felt so dejected and actually knocked on a few neighbours' doors, cheekily asking for a few coins. It was a sad experience.

My mother never possessed much money. My father's wages were in the lowest rate band possible and she made all of our clothes whilst we were youngsters. During my eighth year my mother took Philip and I to relatives who lived on the Wirral coast. She showed us how to collect cockles and mussels and also took us on a bus journey to Fleetwood to find and pester the trawler men for crabs, which she later put into her shopping bag to take home.

One day a large half-dead crab escaped whilst travelling back home on the bus, crawled onto a man's hat in the next seat and camped there. He was not aware, being asleep at the time. The whole bus rocked with laughter. She quickly recovered it and placed it back in her bag. It was bound for the pot. Poor creature. I had no say in the matter.

In order to help out with the household budget my father kept chickens in the rear garden. My mother and father would insist on dispatching me to the houses in the neighbourhood to collect potato peelings which had been left for refuse. These would then be cooked and mashed for chicken feed. I felt rather humiliated when approaching neighbours and asking for their garbage but I was forced to carry out this chore under the threat of a clout if I refused.

I remember one particular house I visited where one of the sons never lost an opportunity to denigrate and ridicule me. I reminded him one day that his father was a dustbin man and was collecting people's potato peelings on a daily basis. He never taunted me again. The message I had delivered proved to be a most effective deterrent.

During this year in January my mother had to enter hospital for a prolapsed womb operation. She was expected to be absent for two weeks. Towards the end of the fortnight, one evening after dinner was finished, I was peering out of the living room window eagerly awaiting her return when she suddenly appeared at the front gate with a neighbour carrying her suitcase. My heart leapt with delight. I loved her so much. My feeling of relief at being close to her once again was indescribable, an uplifting experience, unhappily not too often repeated in the early stages of my childhood.

In the depths of the 1954 winter, I had my first out-of-body experience. Being a typical 'scallywag' I was scooting around the school yard sliding on the ice at full speed. Suddenly I lost balance, hurtled into a brick wall and fell heavily, banging my head on the ground in the process. The next instant I was rising above my body and watching the other children gathered around, trying to awaken my physical shell.

I recall the incident with mixed feelings - being at the same time startled and frightened but also strangely exhilarated and excited. I must have been hovering about twenty feet above in the air but as soon as I started thinking about my body, I felt myself rocketing back into it and recovered consciousness, to find two pals busily slapping my face. The eventual price for my adventure was a throbbing headache that lasted for the rest of the day.

At the time I didn't realise that I was experiencing an out-of-body experience and my schoolmates could not understand my later description of this little journey. I was so full of mischief at this primary school stage. It amazed me how I managed to assimilate or digest any educational information at all.

I took my 11+ examination at nine because of the way my birthday fell during the summer. I passed with a high mark and entered the Grammar School at ten years of age. It was then decided that I should go to a Catholic grammar school but unfortunately, we lived approximately twelve miles away and my mother couldn't really afford the bus fare, so the education department agreed that I could be placed at the Thomas Boteler

Grammar School, where I had heard that Catholics whilst not entirely welcomed with open arms, were tolerated. It was a Church of England school.

My ninth year was coming to a close and I remembered at the time the constant coldness of our house. My brother and I slept together in one single bed; he was placed at the top with myself at the bottom with a large khaki ex-army overcoat covering the two of us. My brother being the stronger, chose the shoulder end and I was left with the cooler bottom end. We slept in a fashion with his feet stuck in my face through the duration of the night and they didn't smell very sweet either but the coat was reasonably warm.

My mother never thought that hankies were a necessity because I was forever wiping my nose on the sleeve of my coat. The shiny reflection was a fixture. Both my shoes usually had holes in them with three or four layers of cardboard packed inside which never lasted very long. Sometimes my feet were left bleeding for hours because I frequently used to walk to school, which was two or three miles distance and kept the two pence which my mother gave me for the bus fare. It was saved to buy sherbets which were regarded as treats. As I didn't have any pocket money, my greatest enjoyment was roaming the countryside, which was, fortunately, free.

At this time paranormal activity was increasing at home, phantom footsteps, frequent voices, knocks, strong fragrances and objects mysteriously going missing and reappearing. These things went on continually and my mother became quite used to it; she accepted it knowing the source was surrounding my father who was a natural psychic.

It was at this time in my ninth year that I began to see colours around people, which were obviously their auras, a discovery which I found most intriguing. I also felt a reassuring warmth at times when I felt very lonely and sad. It was later that I realised that my early brush with death at the age of three had opened up my psychic centres and this was enabling me to read the auras that surround all living creations and also to be sensitive to the spirit world.

The material world was very much a reality and it was thought by my parents that I was too attentive to vermin because I did my very best to save slugs as well as wasps and mice. My mother would insist on pouring salt over them but to me, they were living things, God's creatures; to everybody else they seemed repulsive. Of course they can pose a problem, but still I felt that they too were part of God's creation and deserved the right to live. After all they had not asked to be born.

During this year in the summer holidays, I underwent a quite eventful spiritual experience. This was the occasion when I was taken with my family down to my Aunt Ella's house in St. Albans, Hertfordshire. I remember at that time it was a welcome trip and a very nice place. I settled down quickly but, unfortunately, it wasn't long before I started receiving previously undisclosed information about my Aunt Ella.

There were rooms in the house which were always locked and one morning I happened to close my eyes and immediately saw several bottles of sherry conveniently hidden in the drawers and cupboards. I mentioned this to my mother and never thought any more about it. The next day I asked Aunty Ella, "Why do you keep all those sherry bottles in the cupboards?" My aunt gave me a long, strange look. Into the third day of the holiday she turned around to my mother and said, "Well, I think it is time that Kevin went home. I think it is best for him and me. I just feel uncomfortable with him here." I protested but was soon dispatched back to Warrington by bus, which turned out to be a very long journey.

Afterwards, when my mother returned home, she told me that Aunt Ella had informed her that she had always thought I was rather strange. She also confessed to my mother that she was drinking heavily and was secreting the bottles of sherry around the bedrooms, which I had clairvoyantly seen. I later learned that she was drinking to ease her suffering, brought on by the harsh treatment she received from her husband, my uncle. That was possibly the first time where my clairvoyant psychic senses were opened up - maybe uncontrolled, but it was obvious to me that I knew things that I wouldn't have known. With hindsight, if I had been a little more mature, I would have kept quiet, but at that age, I didn't know any different and was oblivious to the gravity of the situation.

Now into the third year at primary school, it was always the ultimate challenge for the boys to climb to the top of the church tower from the inside shaft which had steel rungs spaced every two feet. The entrance to the church was conveniently attached to the school. On impulse, I finally decided to meet the challenge.

One lunch time, I sneaked into church and found the door to this particular area from where I could climb the tower. I decided to acquire some of the candles that were placed by the statue of Our Lady to enable me to see clearly once inside the base of the shaft. I could then look clean up to the top of the shaft, which I had to climb to reach the base of the spire. Finally I made my successful ascent to the very top of the shaft discovering that the view into the road below was quite magnificent. Little did I know that across the main road from the church, the office staff from the Crossfields soap company were looking out from their windows watching me hanging in and out from the pillars of the base of the church spire. They immediately contacted the Fire Brigade and the police.

The headmaster, Mr Donlevy, was alerted. The next thing I remember was his bellowing from down below for me to come down. I complied with his request as quickly as I could. On touching 'terra firma' I remarked to him "It was quite a climb sir." The headmaster did not look very pleased. His eyes spelled inevitable punishment for me. I was then dragged off to his rooms and given a good thrashing with a cane. What left a deep impression on me was the fact that I was given the thrashing, not for all the chaos I had caused, but mainly for stealing the candles from the base of Our Lady's statue. I considered this to be the typical mentality of a Roman Catholic headmaster; my sin was great! I have since apologised to the Heavenly Father for this incident. I feel sure that he has forgiven me, as I only stole two candles.

During the last summer holiday before I started at the Grammar School, myself and some other rascals were drawn to the irresistible playground which was the American tip belonging to Burtonwood Army Base, just a couple of miles away from my house. To reach this particular dump one had to negotiate many obstacles, iron railings, a railway embankment, railway lines, a bridge, and a wide fast flowing brook (over which was a large cast iron services pipe covered with long spikes which I used to run across with a total disregard for the dangers involved), and then a field full of cow pats presenting the final obstacle before reaching the tip itself.

It was a wonderful feeling moving and rooting amongst all the militaria and discarded uniforms. I carefully chose one and by the time I made my way back to the estate, following all of the other kids. I was now transformed into an officer, wearing an oversized American Captain's uniform, gleaming with insignia. The trouser legs, which I had hitched up, were trailing around my feet nearly tripping me up, but I felt triumphant, an emotion that soon evaporated when I reached home because the smell of the tip was a dead give-away.

My father's reaction was to give me a good belting. He was a big man, 190cm tall, and weighing 100 kilos and he didn't think twice about using his hands. Psychic abilities he undoubtedly possessed, but as far as sensitivity to my pain was concerned, he didn't seem to be aware of it or at least never showed it.

The local canal was also a great attraction in which I used to swim, naked. It was free to use and this fact also appealed strongly to all the kids. It really was a dangerous diseased place to swim , where we actually courted death, as all the local farmers used it to dispose of their dead cattle, poultry and swine. In reality the canal waters were filthy but I loved the swimming and diving. Having no pocket money I could not go to the local swimming baths. Unfortunately, the canal smell used to linger quite strongly and I also got a good hiding for that on reaching home.

One Saturday morning during the school holidays Michael Littler, one of my pals, called at my house to help me clear out the chicken coop and also to conveniently help himself to some produce from the large blackcurrant and loganberry bushes at the bottom of our garden.

We finished the chores quite quickly and were seated having a welcome drink of milk in the kitchen when my mother returned home from the butcher's stall and carefully placed a large sixpenny bag of bulls-eyes on the table. She had purchased them for the purpose of cooking and pressing, which she carried out expertly with the aid of two tin plates and a large flat iron. The end product provided the family with an endless stream of sandwiches which I personally didn't relish but, nonetheless, 'beggars could not be choosers' when it came to mealtimes.

My mother spoke to us briefly and went into the hall to hang up her coat. Michael, unfortunately, could not resist peeking into the bag which resulted in him clumsily dragging it off the table and scattering the eyes all over the kitchen floor. It was an eerie sight as some of them appeared to be staring directly towards us. Michael's face drained and he left quickly through the back door.

I recall shouting to him quite angrily with an air of resignation, "Mike, you rotten swine, don't leave me. You know I will have to face the music!" whereupon my mother returned, saw the mess and was most displeased. "Pick them all up before they dry and be quick", she remarked. It was a most unpleasant task. She cooked them that night. Michael made himself very scarce for a few months - we were never quite as friendly again and I still had to eat some of the finished product over the following week.

CHAPTER TWO

In the late summer of 1956 my first day at the Grammar School arrived. I was to be placed in form B. On the first day the form master soon went around the class asking all the pupils in turn to disclose their father's employment. Various occupations were then revealed including a few doctors and lawyers and other mainly middle class positions. There were only a few of us from working class backgrounds; in fact two of us came from the same Catholic junior school.

When he asked me, I was reluctant to answer because I felt quite sure that he would look upon me differently because of his public school background. This other chap, Ken Earlham, who was with me at the primary school, immediately turned round and said "Sir, I know what his father's job is - he's a labourer, he works on the council and does all the dirty jobs." The master peered at me and remarked contemptuously, "What an interesting pedigree you seem to have my boy." I glared at him with a look of equal contempt and replied "Is that so sir?" The war had begun! I then looked at Ken who had freely given my background to the form master - enough was enough. During break time I gave him a rollicking and he actually apologised, not realising the embarrassment he had caused.

My earliest memories of a religious division at this school was at assembly time in the mornings when three or four of us, who were Roman Catholics, were hustled into a classroom and duly handed a catechism. The door was then firmly banged shut. We were later let out after the normal school assembly had taken place to rejoin the majority.

It was very difficult for my mother during the years I was at the grammar school, because the school uniform was very expensive and then strips for cricket, soccer, and athletics, which were all deemed necessary. My mother used 'Johnny Leigh's', a well known pawn shop to pay off the price of the outfits on a weekly basis.

I had to travel on two buses to get to this school and unfortunately my mother didn't seem to understand the importance of getting me up in time. Inevitably, I used to be late, late enough to earn regular detentions. The number of detentions received also meant further punishments - being caned or whacked across the bottom with sports shoes, a favourite method adopted by our math's master. I was becoming increasingly rebellious - the more thrashings I received, the less co-operative I became. I would not allow my spirit to be broken.

During the early part of my second term, I do recall one memorable incident after school had finished. I was with two of my friends generally fooling around outside the school. A fellow pupil happened to be walking on his way home, past the spot where we were standing. For no reason at all, he looked back and contemptuously uttered, "Ruffians!" My two school pals took umbrage at once, one of them prodded him with a wooden railing that was handy. He didn't injure him but obviously the boy was shaken. On reaching home the boy told his father, who happened to be a local businessman.

The following day the pupil's form teacher hauled my two pals to the headmaster's office and in turn he sent for me, because it was intimated that I had been chiefly responsible for the incident. He commenced with his usual vitriolic tirade about me being an exceptionally troublesome pupil and then promised that he was going to give me a really good caning. I glanced sideways and vividly remember the pleasure in his eyes as he ran about twenty steps and really let fly, six times in all, much too severe a punishment I thought at the time. I didn't let him see that he had hurt me, biting my lip very hard until I got out of his study.

When I got home that evening the caning was very difficult to hide, as I was walking with a gait 'Gabby Hayes' fashion, he being one or my favourite cowboy actors from the old films. My mother immediately knew that something was wrong and asked to see my backside. She shrieked alarmingly, "Kevin, it looks like a union jack flag and it's almost bleeding! You must not let your father see it, because he will travel to the school tomorrow and flatten the headmaster, and probably sort out the other staff members as well!" I managed to hide away from him for the best part of a week before my wounds healed. I didn't wish to make my lot worse than it already was.

During the next day's assembly when I was asked to be present, the headmaster told both staff and pupils about the shameful bullying incident and commented loudly, "That wretched boy McGrath is the most badly behaved and rebellious pupil in the annals of the school's history." His remarks I allowed to go over my head: I deserved better. In my opinion, the headmaster did have much room for improvement with his distant attitude towards the pupils placed at the school, who were regarded as both difficult and disruptive. All I needed was a little more understanding. Maybe behavioural psychologists were about at that time; I only wish I could have had the benefit of their expertise. Maybe I needed to be treated differently because of my home environment, but they would insist on ignoring my obvious cries for help and continued to punish me instead of providing a little more compassion and guidance.

It was now the summer of 1958 and I realised I was becoming far more sensitive to people's moods and thoughts in every way. I was also seeing people's auras far more clearly, I began to realise that I was being summoned for a task far more purposeful which I could not fully grasp, yet instinctively knew was inevitable.

During July I was sent by the sports master, unjustly I thought, to be punished by the headmaster for a prank in the gym. After another typical verbal barrage, we both decided by mutual agreement, or truthfully, he decided that I had no future at the grammar school.

I must add that, on recollection, during my first year at school, I did encounter one kind experience. A school a prefect named Gibson, a tall, red headed chap, during a free lesson came over to me and was very attentive. I felt much kindness within him. He said quietly, "Do you know what son?", he called me son although he could not yet have been eighteen himself. "You are not as bad as they make you out to be. You just need a little bit more encouragement and understanding." I never forgot his comments, they were more or less ingrained into me. Maybe sometime in the future I will come across this kind soul. He didn't realise what impact he would have upon me, even to this day, a few words of kindness from him which were most welcome at the time.

It was not a good year at all because later on, my brother Philip suffered an horrific injury to his right arm whilst working for the Greenall's Brewery, leaving him permanently disabled. After that he fell into a deep depression which was to plague him for the rest of his life.

Further into my teens, at sixteen years of age, I obtained a position in the construction industry with Harper & Finch, Building Contractors. I commenced my working life as an apprentice bricklayer. This enabled me to assist with the family income. I then thought that maybe after I had served my apprenticeship I could later develop a business career.

At that time, the job was conveniently available and did promise some work creativity. It was an outside occupation, ensuring that I would at least be in tune with nature in some say. I preferred not to be enclosed at this time in my life. I soon found out quite early on in this employment that the people involved in it were mostly rough diamonds, but also fascinating characters. I could go on for years about the countless pranks and send-ups, some of them quite crude but also extremely funny, which were perpetrated by my work mates.

Having settled into my first year of apprenticeship - one of my first duties as an apprentice was to collect the fish and chip dinners for the craftsmen and labourers. It took me fifteen minutes to reach the fish and chip shop, and it was obvious that by the time I arrived back, the food would be cooling. The bricklayers accepted this and never complained, but, however much I tried to explain to the leading hodcarrier, that it was not possible to keep them warm, he only replied, "I want the buggers hot!" and proceeded to give me a clip around the ear. This attitude was completely illogical but maybe that was the fascination of those characters; they were never there for long on the site, you might say similar to butterflies, `Here today, gone tomorrow!'

Construction workers were quite loyal to each other, although sometimes insensitive to one's feelings. I didn't really feel comfortable when I was chosen to be insulted during the daily banter; I was very sensitive, although not admitting it to my fellow workers, for they would surely have wound me up even further.

I worked and studied hard however, and soon acquired the necessary craft skills. I was naturally creative when I was at the grammar school, excelling in the artistic subjects. Being stronger in Art, History and Drama. Science, Physics, Maths and Languages were regarded as chores. Later in life I had to study harder in Physics, Science and Maths etc., to gain my professional qualifications. For me it was to prove a difficult undertaking.

I had now moved into my seventeenth year and second year of my apprenticeship. I was apparently regarded as an outrageous character by my work mates and very unpredictable, usually being in the thick of any mischief that was going on. The firm must have suspended me about fifteen times, but my boss, Harold Harper, part-owner of Harper & Finch never sacked me because he knew that I worked hard for the firm and was a skilled craftsman for my age.

Harold Lansky, the General Foreman of the building site I worked on, always gave apprentices a hard time, forcing us in turn to mix concrete by hand for hours at a time which usually left us exhausted. One August day I hatched a plan to get even with Harold. During the evenings he consumed beer on an impressive scale and, conveniently for me, chose to visit the site lavatory every lunch time when nature called.

The lavatory was in the middle of the site and constructed of five corrugated sheets and a door with a small wooden bar fitted inside where one could sit to carry out one's natural functions. As lunch time loomed, I borrowed a saw from one of the apprentice joiners, sped to the lavatory and sawed three-quarters of the way through the seat bar, adroitly disguised the cut with mud and grease and then sneaked off to a nearby house which was part constructed, to join the other boys, whom I had alerted to my prank.

We waited for the foreman to make his daily visit. He did not disappoint us. A few minutes later he ran to the lavatory from his office, carefully negotiating the site rubble and closing the door behind him. Immediately he emitted a hideous scream. The bar had snapped, hurling him backwards into the pit of excrement. He then emerged, in a furious mood, voicing the vilest of expletives, covered from head to toe with the foul contents, accompanied with a sure promise that the whole work force should be sacked to pay for his misfortune. We all found it absolutely hilarious but I knew it would not be long before he tracked down the real culprit and was mightily relieved when Mr. Harper transferred me to one of his other sites to help build house foundations. The old adage was right, 'Don't get mad; get even!' I felt that we were about even.

At eighteen, midway through my apprenticeship I felt I was the finished product as a craftsman, but deep within me, I knew that this was not my true pathway and vocation.

One hot day in August I was helping to build a wall that seemed to be endless, I thought to myself, - "Good gracious Kevin, you can't be doing this for the rest of your life. It is so monotonous - you must find something else." The way I escaped was very painful to say the least. Shortly after my eighteenth birthday, the firm went into liquidation and I was transferred to another local firm, Daniel Cooper & Son. It was not long afterwards that the accident, and subsequent injury to my back happened.

One fine September morning, the boss summoned myself and other apprentices to unload fire surrounds off a wagon. The normal idea was to slowly lower the surround, which weighed approximately 200kgs, onto the operative's back, with two other persons either side to steady it. It would then be placed at a nearby compound.

I reluctantly took my position at the side of the wagon, then catastrophe struck, the two foremen who were lowering the heavy items off the wagon accidentally dropped the fire surround directly onto my spine, the two persons either side of me instinctively jumped away and, somewhat dazed, I staggered forward, carrying the surround before dropping it, suffering excruciating pain. I feel sure that my back would have been broken if I had not been so fit at the time. I vaguely remember crawling and slumping against a house wall and I somehow managed to reach home in a fashion, still suffering great pain.

A friend later telephoned the hospital who advised him to tell me to consult my local GP and to stay in bed. On reflection, they should really have taken me in for an acute examination and treatment. After being off work for a period, I recovered somewhat, but was never quite the same again physically.

The autumn of 1964 was now drawing in and my father gathered the family together one evening and said, "I have to get this off my chest, it's quite disturbing, I have seen a very graphic scene. I am going to die tragically in a road accident. I have been into a trance for a short time and everything has been shown to me clearly. I know the location and season of the year when I am going to be killed, I have seen my body being carried away from the scene. I will try to avoid it but have a duty to let you know now." My mother, brother and sister were all shaken and dumbfounded but I quickly attempted to bury it in the recesses of my mind, relying on the fact that people, however psychic, can sometimes be wrong. Later my mother, brother and sister also appeared to have put it to the back of their minds, probably sharing my sentiments.

During the early part of my nineteenth year I experienced my own first premonition involving the outcome of a horse race. I was a typical lad, drinking, enjoying ladies' company and also having the odd flutter on the horses. Gambling on racehorses was introduced to me quite early because I used to make the slips out for my mother who used to place about fifty horses on one slip known as 'all if cash'. It was amazing, that one could bet thirty to forty horses for threepence. It is virtually impossible to win on this type of bet but she got much enjoyment out of it and regularly I used to put her bets on at the local bookmakers. It was all part of my education - my first insight into gambling.

That autumn I had a clear premonition of the Newmarket Cambridgeshire horse race. I remember 'seeing' the winning horse, 'Lacquer', information which I gave enthusiastically to my work mates the week before the race. They wouldn't believe me and did not pay too much attention to my prediction. My psychic sensitivities were now obviously becoming stronger, but I was also quite naive - I didn't back the horse either and of course it duly won!

This kind of psychic experience also happened to me later in the year. On this occasion the name of the horse `Acharacle' and the jockey Brian Taylor was continually printed on my mind. I scanned the racing pages and waited patiently for it to be declared. Four months later, it finally appeared and was a complete outsider. I scraped together forty quid. How I managed it, is a mystery to this day.

I anxiously made my way to the bookmaker's and placed the bet on at the very last minute. The manager's smile was very expansive. "Good gracious yes, we've got another mug" he must have thought. There was no way he had laid it off either, which was normal practice. That was patently obvious because he was later dismissed by his boss for ignoring this golden rule. He had to pay me £600 winnings because the horse won at 15-1, finishing very fast at the very last moment, winning on the line by a short head. This win enabled me to buy some clothes and shoes and also to treat my mother, buying some furniture and extra food. I did learn afterwards that this foresight is not a regular occurrence; it was to be part of my spiritual development.

It did happen again later on in my twenties when I was shown a sequence of numbers in a dream. Well, as it happened, I was a little too sleepy and next morning, I just couldn't remember the numbers that had been shown to me. I was employed in Local Government at the time. One night, I was shown eight numbers for the weekend pools coupon but could only remember seven. I inserted these onto a coupon with a colleague. They duly came up and I won £450. It should have been the jackpot. Obviously I was meant to be 'dozy' that morning. The jackpot would have interfered with my life purposes, although I was still very disappointed.

On Saturday, the 20th may 1967, my father's traumatic prediction materialised. I was by now twenty years of age, I remember being invited to a friend's 21st birthday. I left the party early because I was working the next day and was walking along Winwick Road. I was not drunk, just a little merry. I remember my head was jerked quite suddenly to one side and looked down a nearby road. In the distance I could see a body lying in the road with much frenzied activity taking place. An ambulance was also present. Instinctively, I knew it was my father for it was the area he had previously insisted would be the place of his death. I quickly ran to the scene by which time he had been taken to the morgue.

I approached a police officer who was still at the scene and he gave me a brief account of what had happened. My father had been crossing the road, which was notorious as a blind spot and had walked halfway across. The traffic was light at the time but a car approached which he obviously did not see. He was struck by the car, fracturing his skull and was killed instantly. I was then taken to the morgue by a policeman. I somehow remained strong during the necessary formal 'identification', which I had to make.

I was later told that at this very moment my mother was upstairs in the bedroom at home when my father appeared to her in spirit form with an obvious head wound. He clasped his hands together and said, "Pray for me." and faded. My mother fainted with shock. He knew the importance of prayer to take him to the other side. It is also a psychic fact, that prayer does help with the transition of a soul that has been forcibly ejected out of the body through tragic or quick death. My father had also appeared to my sister in her bedroom asking for prayer. Although my mother had always been a devout Catholic, her religious education had never prepared her for this spiritual experience. These things were not supposed to happen. It was very soon after my father had materialised, that the news was given to her officially that he had been killed following the road accident.

It was obvious to me that my father was a very powerful psychic and had used his psychic abilities to manifest quickly to get the prayer assistance that he needed for transition to the higher side from his closest earth ties, the family.

During my twentieth year, I enjoyed quite a fun-packed week's holiday at Rhyl, Wales, with my boyhood pals, Patrick Birmingham, Ernie Whiteley and Brian Lovat, memorable mostly for the countless pranks and enormous hangovers resulting from all night drinking sessions.

I also seemed to spend a great deal of time through that summer tending to my father's allotment. It gave me great pleasure to hand out all the surplus vegetables to the pensioners who used to pass by the allotment. There was always plenty available as the chicken compost provided a limitless feed for everything I planted. My mother's kitchen was also very well supplied. It helped her a great deal with the food budget.

CHAPTER THREE

I was now moving closer to my 21st birthday. After several brief liaisons with local girls I met in the pubs and dance halls, I still did not feel like settling down to a serious courtship, preferring to remain free from commitment. when I was 21 I first met my wife, Janet, a tall, pretty blonde in the Lion, a local Public House, when she bustled past me as I tried to get served at the bar. I thought she was a trifle abrasive and to be quite frank while I wasn't very keen on her manner. I was very taken by her good looks. I told her briefly to use her manners a little more often. She did not respond, however, and ignored my remarks giving me a disdainful look. Little did I know that we were destined to meet again; our karmic patterns were to be knitted together for both our earth purposes.

The next meeting with Janet was again in a Public House named the Woolpack. This time I walked in with my friends, a different bunch now, Harry Bird, Dennis Smith and Graham Savage, all good-hearted pals employed in the building trade, loyal but boisterous. I could understand any girl feeling a little vulnerable confronted by lads such as ourselves; our behaviour was not in the least quiet. Janet and her friend appeared a little bit more genteel. When I saw them I suggested, "Let's go and sit near them." I quickly approached her and started making some jocular remarks about her boots being perfect for building work. I was twenty two years old with a natural yearning to fully enjoy myself socially and still intent on remaining single. However, she did make quite an impression on me. We left a short time later.

Our next meeting was in a local night club, the 'Nitespot'. My pals and I found ourselves there one night after trawling round the town's Pubs I spotted her again with Mary, her friend. Close by was a vacant chair, rather awkwardly close to a wall. Janet tried to move it so as to stop me sitting by her. She failed to do so and next to her I sat! We were obviously destined to be together. Janet now fully realises the reason behind the uncanny sequence of events. She later told me that she thought at the time, "If this chair cannot be moved, it must be God's will." As a strong Methodist she had an unwavering belief in God and accepted his will completely.

We courted for about eighteen months and then seized the chance to buy a house which was up for sale in the old Fairfield part of Warrington, near to where Janet lived. To obtain a mortgage I needed a regular job to satisfy the lenders. I then obtained a job with a building firm, Thomasons of Lymm, who held a maintenance contract with Shell Petrochemicals at Manchester. The work conditions were dangerous but work was guaranteed for a long period, which was rare in the construction industry, a notoriously unreliable area of work. My steady job enabled me to obtain a mortgage from the Council. I was working as a maintenance craftsman, seven days a week, with a ten hour working day.

About eighteen months into this contract, one wet day whilst building foundations, I remember a stack of bricks placed above me suddenly began sliding down, rapidly pinning me against the trench. The pain in my back was excruciating, right on the same spot where I had injured it earlier in 1964. My work mates at the end of the foundation did not react quickly and were quite oblivious to my situation. Finally, after being freed by them, I hobbled slowly to the ambulance centre where I was given tablets and advised to go home. My back pain was now quite severe. I had a fortnight off work before returning. I could not afford to stay off for very long, although my injury necessitated further rest. I chose to work on. Although my condition had now become chronic, the payment of the mortgage was of paramount importance.

After a brief engagement, Janet and I married in the Elmwood Congregational Church on 19 December 1970. It was a freezing but gloriously sunny day. She came from a strong Methodist family and I from a devout Catholic family. The church was chosen after careful deliberation; a congregational church was a church of no fixed denomination. It was the ideal compromise as I thought at the time to suit both parties. I was right in my choice as both families were satisfied. Janet and I were quietly pleased that no religious divisions had been caused. After settling into the house we did our best to furnish it with second hand furniture and were happy with the knowledge that one day it would be ours.

It was at this time I experienced the power of thought. I picked up clairvoyantly that one of my circle of friends didn't like me very much. I instinctively knew that he fancied my wife and I was the obstacle. Whenever he found the opportunity he would do his best to antagonise me, being offensive and sarcastic during the time he was in our company. We once visited the Woolpack Public House where he was present. Later he came over to our table and proceeded to make several unwarranted, disparaging remarks. I recall looking at his aura and seeing a strong presence of jealousy. My own aura was probably reflecting red for I felt very angry and I directed my displeasure towards him using destructive thought forms. I realise now that sending such thoughts only appeals to the darker spirits who surround the earth plane, providing them with material for ungodly deeds. A succession of harmful events then occurred around this person quite rapidly. Janet suspected I was responsible and asked me to stop being angry with him, which I did. I realise now when you are psychically sensitive, you can tune in for good or evil.

There was only one other time later in my professional employment that I wished for retribution to be carried out to a fellow soul. I felt very angry towards this man, a work colleague, who was responsible for my working conditions being made difficult. I had meditated strongly on him to receive retribution. I tried to resist it at the time. However, we are only human and I continued to channel my negative thoughts towards him. Thought energy is a potent force. Unfortunately, a person's negative wish is not God's work. My wishes were self-destructive in the long term, however successful at the time.

Whilst still working at Shell Petrochemicals my back condition made construction work increasingly more difficult and most days I was in considerable pain. Eventually I had no option but to leave the construction industry and tried to seek alternative non-manual employment. I found it very difficult to break into professional employment because I had left my education unfinished. Fortunately, I tried hard to seek an opening and after a period of time applied for an education grant through the Common Market as it was known then. This enabled me to take further education at the Clarence College of Building, Liverpool to study for quantity and building surveyor qualifications. It promised to be hard, because it meant total immersion in the disciplines of science, physics and maths which I always hated at school but it was the only way out of my predicament.

Prior to my entry to the Clarence College of Liverpool my mother did write to a renowned healer in London - without my knowledge. At the time I was seeking alternative help to ease and to correct my spinal condition, because I had reached a dead end with the medical profession who didn't seem too concerned with my back injury or reduced quality of life. Although I did put on a brave face it was surprising that even some of the simpler tasks that I had previously taken for granted, I now found very difficult.

Eventually, after about four months, my mother wrote again to the healer who now agreed to see me. I was twenty four years old and I remember travelling by train to London after lunch one day. The journey took two and a half hours. I couldn't sit easily and I remember travelling in great discomfort. I eventually arrived at the healer's rooms in central London. The front door was opened and a middle-aged, bespectacled, well-dressed man, who was smoking a huge cigar invited me in. He walked through the hallway and asked me to follow him into the consulting room.

Before I went in I heard him remark, "I can't heal you through that wall son." There was a record player blaring away in the corner. I thought, this is a strange set-up - noisy record player, Havana cigar, private secretary and very posh rooms. I knew that this wasn't the man for me and that he would not have any impact upon my condition. However, he seemed to have acquired a good reputation as a healer amongst the general Public and the media, hence the reason for my mother having contacted him to help me.

Having travelled so far I allowed him to go through the motions. He placed his hand on my back and said, "You should be alright now son". Maybe others had been helped through him, but I knew quite well that he would not cure me. I paid my £6.00 fee and travelled back on the train, most uncomfortably, the same afternoon to Warrington.

On arriving back I felt somewhat dejected and disillusioned, but my inner faith was not broken. My disappointing visit was part of my spiritual learning, and part of the jigsaw pattern intricately placed in position by God's servants on the spirit side of life. It was to be a vital preparation for the future times when people would be travelling to see me from across the UK with various illnesses. I would ensure that they would be greeted warmly and treated sympathetically. I now realised that my spirit guides had been slowly organising my life in a careful but painstaking fashion.

My studies continued over the next two years while I attended Clarence College. My back trouble made life difficult and I had particular problems with sitting still for long periods and I was constantly shuffling about, unfortunately adding to the tutor's irritation. It was three years of hard slog, necessitating studying into the early hours but I was determined to graduate.

My fellow students were friendly and supportive, even though they were mostly younger than I. We spent our spare hours in the Philharmonic Public House, a quaint civic listed drinking house in the centre of Liverpool, which was usually crammed with students. I enjoyed those times. I finally qualified in 1976 as a quantity and building surveyor.

My academic journey had been very difficult, but I had managed it. I did fail on one discipline - civil engineering. I remember half-way through it, thinking - "Well, enough is enough, Kevin - you have worked hard enough." I felt as though my reserves were well and truly exhausted. It was a pleasant surprise when I finally got my exam results, I had done quite well. At this stage, Janet and I had mostly refurbished our house and it was very cosy. I claimed a front room for my spiritual purposes and my father's rosary was placed over the fireplace where it gave me much strength and comfort.

At the age of twenty nine I recall applying for one particular administrative post, although the money wasn't very good at all. It was for a local pre-cast concrete firm, an off-shoot from a large building contracting organisation. On my way for interview, information was given to me quite strongly, clairvoyantly, that the manager of the firm was irresponsible, a heavy drinker and that he wished to employ me to take on board all his own managerial responsibilities for a meagre salary. I managed to find the offices and went through with the interview, going through the motions as required.

On the surface the manager appeared quite refined, with everything apparently above-board and he offered a secure future for me. Fortunately, I didn't question what had been given earlier to me clairvoyantly and I left, politely telling him that I would consider his offer but in reality did not have the slightest intention of returning.

It was some time later whilst watching a rugby match that I met a young chap who was a bonus clerk with the firm. He said to me, "Why didn't you take the job, had someone warned you about him?" I replied, "No - I just felt that it wasn't right." He said, "Well to be truthful, the boss is an absolute disgrace. Everyone who has worked here, apart from me has left since his appointment. He disappears for most of the day to the Pub, and to be frank, you would have ended up doing his job. It's no surprise everyone leaves so quickly."

I had a quiet chuckle to myself and I said "Thank you" to my spirit friends but felt sorry for the clerk who had to stay because of his own pressing financial commitments. This was the first of many times when the radiant ones who surround me, impinged on my consciousness to help or protect me.

In the latter part of my twenty-ninth year, after numerous attempts to enter the civil service, I finally sought employment in Local Government at Warrington Borough Council as a technical assistant in the Housing Department. The staff turnover in the department was very high. Nonetheless, it was a job and I went for the interview with my qualifications tucked into my pocket. I must have made a good impression as the Principal Surveyor offered me the job directly after the interview. I was quite pleased to gain employment.

Earlier, I had told them about my back condition explaining that I would get by as long as I wasn't expected to sit down for the whole of the day, which caused my back to stiffen up. I passed the subsequent medical, which was required for superannuation reasons, my health perfect apart from the back injury. It was not too long after beginning work in the Housing Department that a senior housing officer made it quite clear that he personally didn't like me too much. I found his aura most informative to this end. I was obviously not 'flattering' him enough.

I had settled into the Local Government office routine and was now aged thirty-one. In the autumn of 1977 I was walking up a nearby street where Bob Hewitt, a local steeplejack lived. I recognised his wife in front of me walking slowly half-way up the street. She was obviously in pain, clutching her arm quite tightly. On closer inspection I saw that she had a large shoulder brace fitted. I felt impelled to approach her and so I walked alongside her and said, "Mrs Hewitt I can see quite clearly that you are in pain." "Yes", she replied. I remarked, "You don't know me very well but I feel you are becoming quite despondent." "Yes" she said "I have got this shoulder problem and have tried every medical treatment possible for three months and it has just not improved one iota, I'm still in a lot of pain." I said "Well, I feel somehow that I will be able to sort it out for you and alleviate your pain." She said, "Do you think you can?" I suddenly received the message clairvoyantly "Yes Kevin, it will be corrected soon." I said to her "Do you mind if I pop in later?" She just looked at me and said, "Alright."

I visited her after tea and requested her to stand directly in front of me and began to prod part of her back slightly with my finger. I immediately saw blue rays streaming directly to a certain vertebra and my hand began to vibrate. I stepped back and then left the house aware that I had done my best and felt optimistic for the outcome.

The next day I 'bumped' into her again. She was walking freely this time, her brace dispensed with. She walked up to me and said, "Kevin, that's your name isn't it? My husband Bob knows you well. I must tell you, the pain has gone." I replied "Has it?" She continued, "Yes, it's completely gone." I looked up to the skies and said "Thanks very much." I realised then that the will of God, through the intercession of spirit, would always have its way.

Before the Christmas holiday I remember a lady colleague, Gill Ellam, bringing her husband, Tony, into the office at the end of the afternoon work period. Gill commented "Kevin, my husband's back is really troubling him, will you please help him?" She knew that I also suffered back trouble. I quietly asked him to sit on the edge of my desk. I then felt drawn to putting my hand on his back. I noticed the healing ray being directed was a clear blue. I reassured him "I suffer the same as you do Tony, please have faith, please trust in God and wait." I finished the healing, bid them both good-bye and went home but I knew something had happened spiritually to correct his condition.

The next day Gill told me "It is incredible, his back pain has lifted. He has thrown his corset away. That is why I brought him to you initially Kevin. I am sensitive to a degree myself and I accept that you may have been able to help him." I was that day in some pain myself but it gave me great satisfaction to heal Tony. The experience also helped to restore his belief in God, which he had lost over a period of time.

CHAPTER FOUR

At each juncture of my spiritual progression, my wife had been simultaneously progressing her working life through a bank and a solicitor's office, eventually ending up in Local Government. She was conscientious and competent at her work and gained first class typing and shorthand qualifications. She, too, was put under unnecessary pressure and eventually moved into the NHS where she really belonged, as she was a natural carer.

On my thirty-second birthday I recall walking past a local book shop and was fascinated by the varied range of paranormal books. One especially caught my eye at the bottom of the bookshelf - it was bright yellow and being a Leo, it attracted me. I picked it up, a book on palmistry. I looked at it and thought, "Yes, this is interesting, I would like to master it." I browsed through it and then thought, "This is impossible, there is no way I can get through this. No, too complex", and then placed it back on the shelf. I walked five or six steps, returned and determinedly assured myself "Yes, I will master this if it kills me." I picked that little book up, bought it and took it home. It had been waiting for me to use it. And that was the beginning of my journey into a very wide range of paranormal, metaphysical and New Age subject matters.

I studied intensely both chiromancy and cheirognomy, the complete sciences of palmistry. I mastered them and read hands for a long time afterwards. I needed much practical experience to become finally proficient in the art of hand reading. I also studied deeply other modes of divination - the tarot, numerology, I Ching, and the runestones. I concentrated on these modes of divination until I had absorbed as much information as possible.

Of all the modes of divination, the one that was the most fascinating and probably worthy of an academic degree was palmistry. It is true that palmistry is a science like astrology and has no association with natural sensitivity to the spiritual dimensions that surround us, but it is very revealing and uncannily accurate.

I looked into astrology for a while only to learn the rudiments. As to the Tarot, when using it, I didn't even have to look closely at the cards; the symbolism alone seemed to evoke my consciousness. I found that one can be a very, very good reader of cards, hands, etc. but there is nothing to describe the wonderful liaison between a sensitive and his spirit guides and helpers.

At the age of thirty-four, I underwent the first of several exhausting tests in hospital due to my back condition. This wasn't thrust upon me: I volunteered. I was in so much pain and discomfort. The first really bad experience was my first radiculogram. I can remember to this day undergoing the lumbar puncture, the huge needle being thrust into my spine, with two burly nurses holding me down. There was no way I could move as they were so strong. Thinking back they would not have looked out of place in a rugby pack! The pain was unbearable but that was only the start. Afterwards, I was left with a dreadful headache and I was probably one in a thousand who was allergic to the substance that had been injected into my spinal canal for the x-ray tests. That was the price of being ultra-sensitive.

My guides have since informed me that my condition was worsened through being allergic to the dye which resulted in my meninges being inflamed. They have also told me that I suffered with inflammation of the spinal nerves following introduction of the contrast dye. (Since undergoing these spinal investigations my lumbar and sciatic pain has actually increased.) I was vomiting for a further three days and then suffered an indescribable headache for a fortnight after leaving hospital, so bad in fact that I couldn't lift my head off the pillow. I felt very ill indeed. It took me three months to recover.

Instinctively, I knew that at some future time I would undergo this suffering again, and so it happened. Three years later I was to enter hospital once more. After being in so much pain, my GP referred me again to the specialist for treatment.

The orthopaedic consultant said, "I think we must have you in again." I entered hospital again and it was suggested, after three weeks on traction which was barbaric and horrific in itself, that I should go through the radiculogram again. The second time was much worse than the first. I do remember the nurses took my blood pressure and tested my pulse prior to the radiculogram taking place. It rocketed. I knew what was in store.

The Consultant said to me afterwards that there were some abnormalities such as a bulged and worn disc and arthritic changes but he didn't think that surgery could be guaranteed to be successful. I was disappointed. I did not complain too much. After all, my back was not meant to be put right. It was not 'God's plan' or at least I consoled myself that, that was the reason for surgery not being offered to me.

It took me four weeks of bed rest to get over this second dreadful experience. I was constantly floating in and out of consciousness seeing various spirit visitors but I knew then that on the other side all they could do was to step aside and allow for my personal choice of treatment which, in hindsight, was wrong. Their task was to make sure that I did not die, which is a possibility any time through illness, especially a serious adverse reaction to an exhaustive spinal investigation.

During the time in hospital whilst I was treated by traction, I took the opportunity of asking the sister to leave me in a single room. It was the only room available as there was no room left on the ward. I gave all the nurses hand readings whilst I was immobile, agonisingly stretched out on a raised bed with two massive weights dangling off my feet. I pleaded with the sister to let me stay in that room. It was a small pleasure to be left alone. I jokingly offered her a palm reading. She laughed and said she was a professional woman but she allowed me to stay in the private room. I decided that I would never again undergo another radiculogram. Given the choice I would rather be executed - less painful I'm sure.

During my thirty-sixth year I was drawn into spiritual healing again, which I had first commenced when I was twenty nine. One chap, Joe Swindells, whom I knew from his work in the building trade said that I actually helped him one night five years earlier while I was talking to him in a local hardware store. At the time he was suffering from a very painful elbow. When I 'bumped' into him shopping during the January sales he said, "You may not know this Kevin but you gripped my elbow and the next morning the swelling and the condition I had been suffering from for three months had gone." He then continued by saying, "I just didn't realise until I thought about it afterwards and I had heard about some of your work. I then realised this was a definite healing confirmation and not a coincidence." This episode of spiritual healing pleased me and provided me with much motivation for the further work to be undertaken.

I continued with my spiritual and psychic activities for the next two years on a decreased level as my mental energies were vastly depleted owing to the unrealistic demands of the post I occupied in the Borough Surveyor's Department, a position to which I had been transferred albeit reluctantly, from the Housing Department.

One beautiful spring morning in 1985, I ran into Mr. Frank Hutson, a local electrical contractor, when he stopped me to ask for a mail order book list. I had known Frank for quite along time and he actually lived nearby. He, on his own admission, had led a wild life. Now he was being drawn to metaphysics through the study of the after-life and hypnotherapy. Also he was very interested in spiritual healing. He wished to increase his learning and at the time was attached to the local Spiritualist church. I gathered that they held a healing circle on a Friday evening and Frank was part of that circle. I think that there were about six healers in all working together.

We started talking about one or two spiritual matters and I knew then that he had been brought into my life so that I could maybe, help him further and teach him more about spiritual truths. I also had a duty to try to develop him to work much deeper spiritually. Later, when he accompanied me on certain spiritual tasks and psychic work, he became a much finer developed instrument as a result of these experiences. He still remains a close friend to this day, although at the present time he is now much more involved with hypnotherapy. He now carries recognised qualifications in this field of complementary medicine.

By this time people were regularly asking me to provide psychic readings. I had to limit the amount of time for these consultations because of my back condition. There was always a proviso that monies for the consultations would be directed to various animal welfare groups. I was associated with many organisations and supported them on a regular basis. These contributions gave me much pleasure as I felt my monies went to a good cause - near to my heart.

Before long however, countless animal welfare charities were asking me for money. I cut my contributions accordingly and felt inclined at the time to send money to other causes; the Mother Theresa Foundation was the first recipient. I didn't realise it at first but Brother Paul, one of my guides, was twisting my arm. It dawned on me that I must also be charitable to my fellow souls and sometimes popped into town to give money to those who were homeless but my interest in animal welfare was still very strong.

It was a kind of reassurance really because I had recently loved and lost a beautiful Siamese cat named 'Lewis', who had tragically been killed. When he initially went missing I was most concerned. He was a favourite of mine, his behaviour almost human. One of his favourite tricks was to open the living room door at will with a lunge of his paws. He went missing for two weeks and we searched everywhere but couldn't find him.

One night I asked for help and my guides responded. A map was clearly shown to me clairvoyantly. I bought a local area layout, my eyes then fastened onto a certain area which began to glow. The area shown was a railway route and I thought, "Good God, that's where he is." The area was covered with snow at that time, about four inches deep. I went to the place and climbed the railway embankment slowly, and with a degree of discomfort, but I managed it. I finally spotted an outline of an animal, half buried in the snow. "Well," I thought, "that's Lewis." I discovered his little body, the poor beggar had been virtually broken in two. I was so upset but comforted myself with the thought that at least I could carry him home and bury him. I brought him home, still awash with tears. I bade my farewell and buried him in the corner of the yard.

However, it wasn't long afterwards that he made his presence felt. His wispy shape was spotted running through the living-room by my niece and her friend. I definitely knew it was 'Lewis' as he had earlier been very clear to me. He certainly loved the house and had returned as quickly as possible to assure me that he was very much alive.

We replaced Lewis with another little waif named 'Susie', a beautiful little grey cat. Lewis appeared shortly afterwards, in spirit form near the fireplace, causing Susie, on seeing him, to adopt an understandable defensive stance - her fur bristled in response. He came back frequently to let me know that he had fully settled and delighted in dossing down in his old familiar areas.

Around this time, I made one or two visits to the local spiritualist church. One particular time, Frank was healing with the other members of the healing circle. I went along out of interest to witness the session. Suddenly, it was very strongly impressed upon my consciousness that I should help a young lady who had attended there to receive healing. My guides were now encouraging me to channel the healing rays as often as possible. I offered my services to Frank.

The lady who was responsible for the healing circle turned to me and remarked icily, "I am afraid you cannot take part in the healing session. No Tom, Dick or Harry can come in here and heal." I didn't argue, just accepted that I would not be able to participate as I wished. "Well, so be it", I thought to myself.

Two weeks later I popped into the church again to watch a medium giving a demonstration of clairvoyance. She said quite firmly, "There is a gentleman here tonight who has been denied permission to provide healing by the church personnel, and by rights he should have been allowed to contribute." I knew then that the higher side had conveyed this information to spur me on in my spiritual works.

Now I had worked for nine years in Local Government on different management levels. In the later stages, as previously mentioned, being removed to another department for the final period of my employment. This situation arose through political manoeuvring amongst higher management and also because one of the senior managers held his own personal reasons for wishing to uproot me from the housing department. Unfortunately, in my changed post, the management wished me to be desk-bound for most of the time. It was quite obvious to me, that my back condition would deteriorate, which it did. It didn't matter which kind of remedial treatment I received the condition worsened.

Eventually I was forced to leave on medical grounds. This was really disheartening for me, considering the fact that I had twice recovered from adversity and was now being beaten, by circumstances beyond my control. I did remember the 'bright ones' conveying to me soon afterwards whilst I was brooding, "The finest steel is always tempered through the fiercest of fires. Keep faith in our great creator!"

I had again struggled through another winter, was enjoying the spring warmth and was now quickly approaching my thirty-ninth birthday. At this time, I came into contact with Jean Robinson, through Frank Hutson, who was quite friendly with Jean at the time. Jean, a recent divorcee, was also quite sensitive and was in the process of developing her mediumship. We had obviously met for a purpose and future events would provide much relevant confirmation.

Late into September after tea, Frank invited me to go to Jean's house. She had been asking him for help to define her sporadic spiritual experiences. He was not too confident in this area and felt I should accompany him. When I entered the house I saw there were many coloured flashing lights around her and there was obviously uncontrolled energy entering the dwelling. I told her that she must develop properly. She wasn't really aware at that time of her proper rate of spiritual development. I knew that the progress should be slow but sure.

A couple of evenings later Jean telephoned me and said that she had climbed into bed and was just about to drop off to sleep when she was awakened by the blanket being dragged off. An evil smelling male presence appeared and began to fondle her. The spirit, although not fully formed, was extremely menacing and unpleasant. Not surprisingly, she was reduced to a state of total panic and did not sleep in the bed for the next few nights, preferring to sleep in the armchair. She was so frightened that, eventually she went to stay in a caravan which belonged to one of her relatives. She telephoned me from a Public telephone kiosk and informed me that the discarnate entity had subsequently followed her to the caravan. I agreed to help and she eventually returned home. I felt that whatever the presence was, it was malevolent, and had to be dealt with as such.

Whilst concentrating on my preparation for the problem at hand I realised that during my early spiritual awakening, I had been impelled to read as much as possible about the life of the Master Jesus and his profound teachings. In particular, the powerful messages conveyed through his disciple St. Paul in the Corinthian epistles of the New Testament, carrying much encouragement for the natural psychics of future ages. These truisms were to provide me with much support, as the spiritual tasks I had taken on board for my incarnation were slowly materialising. This situation concerning Jean was a typical example to test my faith and resolve and I was determined not to be found wanting.

After a period of meditation and prayer, I fed Susie, my cat, pitched her out for the night and popped down to Jean's house. I approached the situation by telling her, "This is a gentleman who maybe a lower spirit in nature, but nevertheless he is still a child of God. However, he will have to be dealt with in a strong manner." Then automatically, I uttered the commands that were needed. I thought at the time, there was no middle ground, he would have to be moved over to the other side of life, to his rightful place where he belonged. This was soon confirmed because I felt the atmosphere change at once from sheer coldness to a reassuring warmth that permeated right through the bungalow.

The next night Jean telephoned me again and confirmed that everything was fine with no problems. I still felt that she was vulnerable as she was still psychically developing and was unfortunately a beacon for the inferior denizens of the astral plane, who are always bent on mischief. A developing medium is always at risk in this respect and Jean was still attracting some 'riff-raff'.

Once again, it wasn't too long before another character was drawn to her. The troublesome spirit regularly moved her furniture and make-up and systematically rearranged her curtains, appearing at will. He had previously lived during Cromwellian times as I had seen him dressed accordingly but nevertheless he was earth- bound and very much in need of resettling to his rightful spirit dimension. Again I carried out the necessary procedure of exorcism and peace was restored.

The next step in Jean's development was a little unusual. Her father, who had died a few years earlier was brought in as her guide and control. I felt that this situation was only temporary and this proved to be the case as in her later years, a lady guide named 'Pearl' was assigned to her for the rest of her mediumistic term.

During November Jean contacted me again. At the time I hadn't been feeling too well physically and my nervous system was quite debilitated. Jean's twin sister who lived in Appleton, was separated from her husband, also had a few health problems, chiefly caused by depression, and psychologically it was a very trying time for her.

In a most frightened state Jean's sister reported seeing a big black shape appearing upstairs which had proceeded to start pushing the children down violently onto the bedroom floor. I thought, "Good heavens, what is going on here." Feeling ill, I decided to give clear instructions to Jean over the telephone how to deal with the matter. I still felt absolutely dreadful but I quickly reflected, "There is no way I can allow her to carry out this work on her own." I rang her back a little later and told her not to worry, I would travel down and sort out the problem. She replied, "It's OK, I have already made arrangements to pick you up. I knew that you would carry out this exorcism personally." My father had told me clairaudiently, "Don't worry," he said, "Kevin is coming whether he is ill or not." So she had been alerted from the higher side about my intended intercession. I then made my way to the house.

When I arrived I could sense the malevolent spirit presence. I gave Jean a silver crucifix and chain to wear as I felt strongly that she would need extra protection whilst I carried out the necessary removal of the evil spirit. I had earlier prepared for my protection and proceeded to go and investigate throughout the house. I quickly saw the dark male spirit on the ground floor and he knew of my intentions. He gravitated up the stairs and I followed. Although I was not feeling well at the time my concentration was still very strong. It had to be, for this malevolent spirit was obviously strong, therefore my concentration had to be one hundred per cent in order to effect his exorcism.

As I was blessing the bedrooms, he moved from one room to another. There were five bedrooms in this detached house. I finally entered the last bedroom and cornered the entity. I mentally told him: "Move no further. You will have to be resettled elsewhere." His eyes glared back at me, they were not too co-operative! I carried out the exorcism procedure asking for the most powerful spirit assistance. I saw the colours around this lower spirit; the guides were forcing him through the astral gateway at full power and obviously escorting him to his rightful place.

The procedures had been carried out fully in accordance with spiritual law and the ultimate will of God, that is why the exorcism was successful. God's laws are perfect and always prevail. Above all, the children were psychologically at risk. The spiritual operation was of paramount importance.

Jean and her sister then collapsed onto the settee. Jean's father then contacted her from the higher side and said, "That's better, it was needed." Then he added, "Strangely enough we can't do it from our side, we have to work through those in the flesh to carry out such important spiritual transition." I welcomed a great sense of relief and also felt that I was executing spiritual work which many mediums will not get involved in, or are not too keen on the responsibility required for the procedures. That gave me much satisfaction.

Jean then handed back to me the small crucifix and chain which I had earlier asked her to wear for extra protection. My advice was not misplaced as on examination it was found to be noticeably bent, indicating that, in desperation a final, unsuccessful attempt had been made to attack her by the evil spirit during my conduction of the exorcism. Later, on reaching home, I returned the crucifix to its normal place over the hall doorway. It never failed to remind me that the universal power can also be utilised through darker forces in contrast to the pure spirit helpers and guides channelling it for Godly reasons. To this day, there has never been a repeat of any spiritual disturbance at the house.

Beginning from the year of 1977 and up to and including the year of 1987, the animal welfare organisations were still the chief recipients of donations given from my readings. My enthusiasm for psychic readings remained and the feedback I received later from persons who consulted me was very encouraging. People were usually quite pleased that predictions that I had made for them were proving extremely accurate, although I was always very careful how I couched advice concerning future illness. It was of most importance to me to be responsible and not to cause too much alarm. One should never provide a fellow soul with a primed time-bomb of a future date of illness.

My spiritual work, however, was the most important aspect of my life. In the July of 1987 Frank Hutson again telephoned me one evening and told me that a young lady named Deborah Mills had met him and taken the opportunity to give him the outline of her problem which was a haunting at her house. He immediately told her to contact me advising her that I was the person best equipped to deal with the matter. Debbie contacted me soon after and I prepared for the spiritual work that I knew would be required. Frank agreed to provide me with a lift to her house.

Three days later I remember arriving at the troubled dwelling, situated on Manchester Road, Warrington. Deborah's late boyfriend, Anthony, had died through a tragic accident twelve months earlier. He had asphyxiated on his own vomit after a bout of drinking. Another boyfriend, Mark, had since moved into the house with her, they had settled nicely into a firm relationship but suddenly strong psychic phenomena began to take place. This was very scary for the couple. Usually, unless I was informed through the higher side to the contrary, I always kept an open mind when I was first asked to investigate. I was informed clairvoyantly, however, that this haunting was genuine.

Immediately, as I entered the upstairs room I felt a male spirit presence. He then quickly materialised, his face showing a blank expression and he was obviously very sad. He communicated to me that he didn't want to leave Deborah and that he was a little jealous of her new relationship with Mark. These strong feelings had fastened .him to the earth plane. To remove his unhappiness, I knew that the surest way was to guide him to his rightful place in the spirit realms. The remedy was not to be exorcism but rather a question of asking for divine help to gravitate him to the higher side. I carried out the necessary ceremony, blessed the dwelling and from that moment on peace prevailed.

Some nine years later it was reported to me that Deborah had travelled to London on holiday where she had consulted a medium. During her sitting the medium immediately brought Anthony through. He again confirmed his name and spoke to Deborah through the medium asking, "Why are you contacting me now? Can't you see, I am quite happy where I am. I did not wish to leave the earth plane before but Kevin helped me to settle where I am now, so please, leave me alone. I assure you that I am OK, please get on with your life and with your new man." Deborah was quite shocked by this experience. However, for me it further proved the power of the spirit intelligentsia on the higher side.

On reflection there was no way that particular medium could have known about the circumstances and events that happened before between Debbie and Anthony, including my intercession.

Also further evidence had been provided that this male spirit had eventually settled down when taken to his rightful place in the spirit planes, albeit reluctantly at first.

At the back end of the summer from time to time I was visiting people in the locality giving spiritual healing, especially to the elderly who couldn't get out. One particular old chap I visited had always been a keen snooker player, but his hands were now gnarled with arthritis. I gave him healing on three occasions. When I visited him on the fourth occasion he had regained much use of his fingers. He was really thrilled. There was no fee involved for my services, it was a privilege to be able to improve his condition. Before I finally left, I remember him remarking, "I'm off to Thames Board Club to resume my snooker!" The bright look on his face was ample reward for me.

CHAPTER FIVE

I knew that I had spirit helpers but I wasn't aware of who they were for a long time, only that they were quite knowledgeable and powerfully effective. Then, for me, the most enlightening experience of my life occurred when they finally introduced themselves to me during the October of 1987.

Frank Hutson, his partner Klaasje, Janet and myself went along to the final demonstration at the local Spiritualist Church where a nationally renowned medium, George McAllister, had been booked to demonstrate his mediumistic clairvoyance for the week. During the two previous demonstrations I attended, the medium had been chosen to give me vital spiritual information.

The demonstration commenced, he then pointed to me and told me that I had a North American Indian with me, at my side, and I also had two other guides. I thought, "This is truly pleasing. At least now I'm being given the kind of information which is most important to me. I may now be able to relate personally to those guides who are with me." He further revealed to me that one of my helpers, my premier spirit guide was a Franciscan monk and the other two spirit guides were a North American Indian and a Chinese physician.

That same evening after the demonstration had finished, Janet visited a friend and I made my way home to finish some correspondence. Later whilst writing in the living room, as the parish church struck ten o'clock, I began to experience a very high-pitched whistling sound in both ears and felt an invisible grip on my arm, lifting me gently to my feet. A powerful presence of power quickly filled the room and the unmistakable outline of a spirit figure began to take form. 'Red Feathers' came through first, resplendent in his war bonnet, confirmed his name immediately and said, "Now is the time for introduction and together we will continue to deal with the many souls that need to be healed. Do not worry," he said "I will see to them, through you." He was very colourful in appearance and also very incandescent, he then stepped back and faded.

A commanding hooded figure in a glowing habit then materialised, obviously a monk, who gave his name as 'Brother Paul' of the Franciscan Order. He said, "We have been with you since birth Kevin. When you fell seriously ill as an infant we ensured that you did not come over to our side. We didn't want you at the time, you had a special job to carry out. There are so many souls for you to tend to. There is a chosen mission for you in your life. Hence the reason for the non-healing intercession from the higher side for your back condition, allowing you to fully empathise with your fellow souls suffering pain and anguish. For our purposes you will prove to be a more effective instrument." This communication was a wonderful and comforting experience. He then made the sign of the cross, blessed me and stepped back.

Another bright spirit form then materialised dressed in traditional Chinese robes and gave his name as 'Dr Wan Chan'. He wrapped his arms, looked towards me and said, "I am assigned to you chiefly for your development of clairvoyance." Then Brother Paul stepped forward again and said, "I will help you with the necessary exorcisms, soul rescues, and other very strong spiritual work that you will be called upon to execute. I will protect you at all times. May I inform you that on earlier occasions when you have carried out spiritual clearance work, I have been in close attendance without your knowledge. He continued "We must utilise an earth instrument to carry out God's wishes in this respect and you agreed to be our instrument before birth."

Red Feathers then materialised again and commented, "Yes, I will be responsible for the direction of the healing rays and associated clairvoyance. We have plenty of work to do Kevin." Then Dr Chan again - he just wished to be called Wan Chan - began to speak, very quietly, "And I am here to make sure that you psychically unfold properly, increasingly so as you move on with your tasks. Time is of the essence," he said, "but just trust in us, trust in God the Father. Your duty started some time ago, we have been with you since birth and we will be with you until your time of passing."

I thanked them, gripped my pocket crucifix tightly, looked at each one in turn and replied, "Messages received and understood." I knew at that moment that I would always be committed to my spiritual mission. They each, in turn, slowly faded and left my presence. The buzzing sensation I had been experiencing throughout the messages also stopped. I went to bed feeling completely elated.

Later in life, when I was giving absent healing to various people in different parts of the UK and overseas, people who were themselves sensitive, who had contacted me for assistance, verified that they had clairvoyantly seen my spirit guides, whilst receiving healing. My guides understand me fully and there has never been a time no matter how difficult the situation I went into that I could not rely upon these bright souls completely for direction and protection. I also knew that I had travelled out of my body through astral projection to carry out reconnaissance of the haunted dwellings that had to be attended to, always accompanied by Brother Paul. So preparation, in spirit form, was frequently made before soul rescue or exorcism was undertaken, some days earlier, before I attended in person.

Careful preparation also had to be made prior to moving into any situation where exorcism was needed. I always prepared firstly by spending a short time in church. I usually preferred to attend a Catholic church in Warrington, it was very effective for exorcism and soul rescue purposes. I used to visit during confessional time, when it was usually quiet. Once or twice when I entered the church during this period, one of the nuns who was attached to the church tried to usher me out. It must have been due to my dark stubble and 'Romany' appearance.

One Saturday morning on visiting the church, after I had collected some holy water for future usage, I went to put some money into the overseas missions box. I spotted a nun over my shoulder and immediately picked up her thoughts. She was thinking "This man is trying to steal money." I was aghast, turned round and said to her, "Excuse me, I am not stealing anything.

53

I'd rather be executed than steal money from a church." She began to blush profusely because she knew that what I had said was correct. She replied, "Oh no, I would not think that son, not in a million years. You are welcome here. What would be your name?" I told her. "By God," she said" that's a fine Irish name, you must be a Roman Catholic. Go on, you are OK." Underneath, however, I knew that she felt a little ashamed of her previous thoughts. The prime objective of my visit was intense prayer to the Heavenly Father and Jesus Christ. This preliminary action would form an integral part of all my soul rescue and exorcism works.

My guides have informed me that the Master Jesus still has enormous influence over the earth plane and the advanced souls still periodically travel to the higher realms to listen to him, and to bask in his radiance. Protection for my aura was of paramount importance. When one enters a haunted dwelling or premises, the lower spirits are aware of your aura and will attempt to breach it. I was well aware of this fact which necessitated strong preparation before I entered any dwelling or premises where strong malevolent forces required removal. I always used a prayer which gave me protection for the required time to conduct an exorcism or soul rescue.

There were many different times when I was consulted to resolve haunting problems. The people requesting remedial action usually didn't wish for any Publicity at all because they were concerned it may influence future house purchasers and because they didn't want to be regarded as odd by their neighbours and friends. Nonetheless the transition of some very unhappy, lost and confused souls was carried out frequently as was the successful ejection of many powerful malevolent entities with complete discretion assured.

One supernatural episode during the January of 1988 that I distinctly remember, involved Frank Hutson's son, Kieran, who happened to be very sceptical of the spirit world. A boisterous chap and physically very powerful being a club bouncer in his spare time. However, whenever spiritual matters were discussed he appeared uneasy and a trifle frightened.

He entered the bathroom one evening, locked the door behind him to keep out his children and began to have a shower. Suddenly, he was punched hard, twice, in his back although he was alone. He told his father about this incident which had really alarmed him. Frank immediately contacted me. I asked the higher side for assistance and was promptly given the relevant information that I should look for a large yellow lamp in the house. That was where I would find the source of the spiritual problem, which happened to be a malevolent force.

One week later, after careful preparation, I visited the house. Sure enough, a large yellow lamp was placed at the top of the staircase. I looked up the stairwell and saw a dark hostile apparition. It didn't wish to reveal itself fully but it was reacting angrily towards me because it knew that I was intent on removing it. I carried out the necessary procedure quickly. As I made my way back downstairs an obnoxious smell streamed past me and travelled rapidly down the staircase. I was beginning to feel nauseous and actually opened the front door to let it out.

The experience had left Kieran deeply shocked, Frank had also smelt the odour and was now satisfied that his son and family would be safe from any further spiritual disturbance. I felt sure that young Kieran was also psychically sensitive although he didn't realise it. He had been undergoing a lot of stress at work and was giving off a air amount of psychic energy and consequently, unknowingly, he had attracted this inferior spirit into his home. His sparkling aura had acted as a beacon on the astral plane and this, unfortunately, does sometimes attract troublesome discarnate spirits.

The weather of April 1988 was pleasantly warm and for a week or two I concentrated on further restocking my treasure trove of books at home. They were very important to me. At this time Frank Hutson had bought a bungalow as an investment but, after a short time, decided that for financial reasons he would have to sell it. During the interim period it was used as a healing sanctuary and some very powerful cases of healing intercessions were carried out which I shall describe later.

Later that month a very important spiritual task was to be undertaken. It commenced with Frank, who was operating in the healing circle one Friday at the local Spiritualist church. A young lady was brought into the church. She was most distressed. Her parents had brought her to the church in the hope that the members could help out with her acute anxiety state and depression. It transpired that she had been treated by a psychiatrist for various mental conditions, when it was to be proved later that she was being plagued by inferior spirits. Obviously, the hospital thought that she was suffering from a form of schizophrenia or neurosis. Frank strongly suspected that it was an issue far more complex than the condition the psychiatrist had earlier diagnosed. He also thought that the young girl might not receive the necessary assistance which was being requested by the parents at the church.

Frank immediately contacted me at home. My guides informed me that an exorcism was necessary. I, in turn, contacted her parents. They had previously heard about my spiritual work and they also welcomed my intervention, so a time was chosen for me to attend. I made arrangements with Frank to pick me up to visit their home two days later. I remember at the time we had been having a lot of inclement weather. After making my preparations Frank picked me up to travel to the house, which was located in Orford, one of the sprawling estates surrounding Warrington town centre.

Suddenly an almighty storm broke out. I thought it was quite ominous. Also, whilst journeying in the car we both experienced a blast of air. I knew quite well that the dark forces were trying to keep me away. The impact forced my head backwards and to make matters worse I was already leaning on my side to accommodate my back problem. Frank's grip on the steering wheel was simultaneously loosened, almost causing him to lose control. This powerful blast of air could not have been referred to as a natural phenomenon. Notice to back off had been served from a supernatural source. A little ruffled, we carried on with our journey to the house.

We were a few hundred meters from our destination when we spotted another car travelling in the opposite direction. The car suddenly swerved into the path of our vehicle, forcing Frank to slam on the brakes. It made a full circle and finally stopped directly in front of us. The male driver climbed out, shaken and quite apologetic. I clambered out and reassured him, "Don't worry mate, it's not your fault." He seemed most bemused. From the darker side of the astral plane efforts were obviously still being made to prevent the exorcism. We continued onwards, reached the house and were invited in. The young girl was sitting alone in the living room. I investigated the whole dwelling which seemed to be seeping with malevolence.

My guides were impressing on me that firstly I should go upstairs. As I went into the bedroom I saw, clairvoyantly, quite large dark spirit forms, there were at least three. It had been reported that the girl had frequently heard several voices during the night-time. She had not been imagining them. The entities appeared quite ugly and were of an inferior spiritual nature.

They had previously been attracted through ouija-board activities some years earlier. The use of ouija-boards can be dangerous, operating as a beacon for inferior spirits who gather on the astral plane. The very thought of wishing to communicate attracts them and they will stoop to profess to be The Christ himself to gain the sitter's confidence. As far as I am concerned it is not healthy to use them.

I proceeded with the task. With Brother Paul directing the power, I carried out the total blessing of the house. The exorcism of the lower spirits which was necessary, was also carried out. I then concentrated on the girl and carried out a certain procedure to cleanse her aura. I also wanted to reassure her that the particular characters who had plagued her for years had been dealt with and removed. I mentioned that it might be necessary for me to return to the house for further attention.

Sure enough, I was informed a few days later that there was still poltergeist phenomena taking place. I thought "Well I must finish the job properly." I returned and this time there were no obstacles. I went through the house, cleared the residual psychic energy and information was then given to me clairvoyantly that the problem was now resolved. I then left, somewhat relieved.

Some time afterwards, my wife, Janet, met the girl's sister who remarked to her "Well, I have been a sceptic all my life, but I must admit that from the second time Kevin visited, my sister has been fine. I wouldn't have believed it, if I hadn't seen the change in her for myself. Everything at home now is quiet and peaceful."

This haunting experience filtered through to the local press. Mr McCauley, a local journalist, contacted the family and subsequently featured the experience in the local Guardian newspaper. When he interviewed me I insisted that the family remained anonymous. He agreed that they had suffered enough. I did notice that when I was carrying out this form of spiritual work I was always punished in a fashion, mainly with electrical appliances at home being strongly affected.

After one exorcism I had carried out, an expensive Sony video recorder which we had bought would not function properly. The channel dial was fluctuating in a very strange way. The Sony engineer was brought out because it was still under guarantee. He arrived and closely observed the programme panel where the channel dial was still rotating wildly. He seemed to lapse into a state of shock and turned rather pale remarking loudly, "Good heavens, I'm afraid I can't handle this. I have never encountered a malfunction like this before." He then made a feeble excuse, put his tool case away and disappeared rapidly. I realised that this was the work of inferior spirits interfering materially to unsettle me. I decided then to send the video down to my mother's home so that my niece could use it. Sure enough, on arrival it worked 'like a dream' as soon as it was switched on and has been functioning normally ever since.

A month later I was well wrapped up owing to a cold, wet snap. I was still continuing my psychic activities with people periodically visiting my house for healing, many with back problems. Fortunately, I managed to address their conditions with a great deal of success, Red Feathers and Wan Chan being chiefly instrumental. They were very effective. The spinal problems were usually described to me through clairvoyance. The information was supplied by Wan Chan. Red Feathers would then take over. In a matter of one to five minutes their backs would receive healing and the majority were successfully treated. In many instances the usual array of expert treatments had already been pursued, including physiotherapy, orthopaedic traction, osteopathy and chiropractic treatment without success. To be chosen as the final link to cure them gave me great satisfaction.

As time progressed, I was to deal with almost the complete range of physiological conditions. Although my own condition restricted me somewhat there was never a time when I refused a healing request. I was obviously given energy when required and whenever I needed extra power it was always granted to me.

June arrived and it was still too wet for my liking, I preferred frost, at least it was dry. The telephone rang one Saturday morning with a request for healing from an Iranian lady who lived in London. Her friend, a northern lady, Patricia Hassey, had advised her to contact me. She was due to have an operation which was to be carried out privately for a severe case of fibroids in her womb. She was desperate, however, to avoid surgery. I asked my guides in the usual manner for help with the lady's condition. It was a difficult time for me also because I was going through an acute phase of sciatica which had caused me to hobble around the house in severe pain for most of the time. However, arrangements had been made which I intended to honour.

She arrived three days later with Patricia, whose mother lived in Runcorn, Cheshire. On her arrival I thought "I can't spend too long with this lady." My sciatica was causing me considerable pain. Nevertheless, I managed to place my hands on the area where she was having the problem. My guides informed me that all would be well, I saw the strength of the healing rays. I took my hand away after a short while and commented, "Well, that's it love. Off you go." She quietly closed the door behind her and left. I then flopped back onto the living room floor to ease my discomfort.

The next day Patricia, who had advised her to consult me, rang from London and said, "Well Kevin, you have done the trick. She is now one hundred per cent improved and has actually cancelled the operation following the all clear from her specialist." My wonderful spirit helpers had been responsible but they knew during the healing session that I was uncomfortable and in pain. Maybe I had sinned greatly in my previous lives. The laws of 'Karma' had always appealed to me as the logical answer for suffering.

CHAPTER SIX

Frank Hutson was still using his bungalow for healing purposes and periodically asked me to pop down. I agreed to do this but only for short periods of time. It was a sunny August day. Frank rang and informed me that my services were being requested by people who had arranged to travel for treatment. I made my way to the bungalow by bus and chose the front room for the healing work required.

The first lady to enter gave me a surprise, or was it a surprise? It was Mrs Hassey, the mother of Patricia who had brought down the Iranian lady. Mrs Hassey walked very stiffly into the bungalow, obviously in much pain suffering from a whole range of conditions including a spastic colon, slipped disc and an ulcerated stomach. I immediately placed my hands on the different areas of the body in turn and I could see my spirit helpers around me directing the healing rays which I noticed, were purple, orange and blue. I knew that strong healing was taking place.

A matter of minutes passed, then she straightened up, her eyes were locked into mine and I could see that she was getting positive relief. She then began to cry and uttered shakily "I can't believe it, I just can't believe it. The pain has gone. I knew I had to see you Kevin." She left the bungalow much relieved, got into the car and I thought "God's will has prevailed."

The next chap to come in from the other room was Bill Gaskell from Runcorn, Cheshire. He came in with his head bent very low. He was quite thin and cut a really sad, pitiful figure. As I got closer and looked at his neck I saw a scar, which showed that he had undergone a serious operation. It transpired that surgery had been necessary to remove six worn discs. He had been in constant pain following the operation and was deeply depressed. The only reason he had come for healing was due to the fact that his wife who weighed about sixty kilograms had dragged him there! He had no religious beliefs at all and so he was extremely sceptical about the benefits of faith healing. I then asked my guides, "Please relieve his pain."

I placed my hand on his neck, I again felt the heat, saw the rays flowing freely and felt optimistic. I didn't spend too long with Mr Gaskell, maybe five minutes. I then removed my hands and Bill automatically moved his head back. We were both jubilant. His pain had finally been lifted and I thought "Good gracious, we have got two instantaneous cures here; there must be some reason for it." I accepted that it was God's will and carried on.

Another chap came in. I thought "Kevin, this will be your last healing treatment." I could feel myself stiffening up and shuffling around uncomfortably. The man's name was Mr Donaghue, also from Runcorn. He had a very bad eye condition. I gave him healing for a short time. I was later informed that his eye condition had improved significantly. Pat Hassey's sister, Mrs Cox, suffered from arthritis and was in much pain, and although I had intended to finish my healing for the day, I was prevailed upon and managed to attend to her for a short period. She also felt relief from the acute pain of her condition.

My spirit guides broke in and informed me "Kevin, through your own suffering we are now able to channel much stronger healing rays and, hopefully in time, we can lift them further!" Frank Hutson was also giving healing to people in the other room. He said afterwards that those he had tended had remarked on the benefit received. I was pleased for them and for him as he was committed to his healing work.

I now fully understood and realised the power of absent healing. People from different parts of the world would obtain my telephone number from the Psychic News Publications and I would act on their requests for spiritual healing. The distances involved were sometimes quite far, from the West Indies to New Zealand and Australia. Obviously these people could not get to me, but the Bright Ones who worked through me on the higher side travelled to them and treated them accordingly.

A young lady from the West Indies wrote to me asking for healing assistance for her skin condition. I asked my guides and helpers to attend to her. In an instant I knew that they were at her side. I received information by letter not long afterwards that the necessary healing and subsequent cure had taken place.

I then realised the effectiveness of distant healing and to this day it has formed an integral part of my work. Contact healing is always very satisfying because one has personal contact with the person who consults you, but above all, the overall process of healing is the only consideration, contact or absent.

On the afternoon of a warm September day I was watering my favourite 'Jackmanii' clematis when Sue Knowles, the manager of the Rope and Anchor Public House at Woolston, Warrington, informed me that her husband, Ron, was bed-bound with a severe back injury. The Orthopaedic Consultant had been called out to see him and stated that he must stay in bed for at least a month with his injury. She asked whether I could do anything to help as it was very important to the running of the Pub for Ron to be back on his feet as soon as possible. I made arrangements to go down to the premises the following evening.

On arrival at the Pub, I slowly made my way upstairs to the bedroom and was faced with a burly figure lying on the bed, grimacing in pain. I thought "I may get this chap right, but it's going to be difficult." I made a request for him to move closer to me but he somehow managed to roll off the bed and dropped onto the floor with an almighty thump and I was afraid that the regulars drinking downstairs would be interrupted with him hurtling through the ceiling!

I carried out spiritual healing and felt his vertebrae move. I then asked him, "Please try to stand up." "That's impossible," he replied. "You must," I reiterated, because Red Feathers was telling me his spinal column was now adjusted back to normal. He then stood up and said, "Kevin, I am amazed." I replied "Ron, it isn't amazing, you have been healed through God's will." Sue thanked me and I then left the premises. I had been instrumental in being in the right place, at the right time. Quite simply, Ron Knowles was meant to be healed. The regulars were not displeased either.

During the last days of September before Frank sold his bungalow I agreed to pop down one Saturday to carry out a few healing treatments. A young girl arrived for healing forwarded by a local tarot reader, Dorothea Miles. She had a very serious back injury and was shortly supposed to enter hospital for surgery. Red Feathers interceded again. Her back was re-adjusted and she was cured. They were perturbed on the higher side as her condition had been wrongly diagnosed in the first place. That particular day I was in some discomfort myself and regularly had to lie on the hard floor between healing sessions. I thought at the time, "Oh for a rubber floor." It would have indeed been most welcome.

The next person to enter the room was a Pakistani lady. She must have weighed about ninety kilograms, and painfully struggled into the room using two walking-sticks. Apparently she had been involved in a road accident. The hospital said they couldn't improve on her treatment. She had suffered a whiplash injury, her spine had been jolted, severe bruising was evident and several of her discs had been compressed. I remember approaching the lady and it was suggested to me by Red Feathers that the best way to cure the problem was to simply hug her tightly and leave the rest to Dr Chan and himself. Although extremely difficult for me, I somehow managed it and everything just seemed to click back into place and she left walking freely. However, I paid the price, suffering badly with spinal pain for the next three weeks.

I remember many years earlier that a similar situation occurred when I suffered physically after applying healing. I had been giving healing to a lady suffering from MS. She began to draw magnetic healing from my aura causing me to feel quite ill. This was the first time this had happened to me and it was also the last because the purest healing takes place through spirit healing. Since then I have never failed to be invigorated after spirit healing but to develop properly we must all go through our apprenticeship. We all make mistakes in the early stages of

CHAPTER SEVEN

November 19th was a date that brought an experience which was both chilling and enlightening. For some considerable time since my late twenties I had periodically left my physical body, chiefly between midnight and 3 am, and travelled freely through the astral plane. The journeys had always been pleasant as I explored scenic countryside and mountain ranges. However, on this day, which was a Sunday, I had been reminiscing, stoking up old grudges towards old work colleagues who had been instrumental in making my working conditions most difficult whilst I was employed in Local Government.

When I retired to bed Janet was already asleep, having gone earlier to gain a more restful night's sleep for the Monday's usual heavy workload which awaited her at the start of the week. I dropped off into a light sleep and was soon woken up by a hand stroking my forehead. I focused on a dome of brightness before me. Brother Paul then materialised, his voice was quiet but firm. "Kevin I have been tuning into your thoughts today. I understand your natural feelings of anger but now is the appropriate time to take you beyond the astral plane and show you a different end of the spiritual realms which reflect such negative vibrations." Whilst listening intently, I had unconsciously left my physical body and was now ascending slowly, following my guardian spirit.

I soon entered the astral plane with which I was familiar and felt comfortable, yet was being drawn quite strongly and magnetically towards an area which was much dimmer. I could see Brother Paul, whose spirit colours were always radiant, at my side. The scenery was becoming very drab now and the atmosphere much cooler, with no plants or foliage evident and the light much weaker. I now found myself slowly walking on a descending uneven road which seemed to be endless. The surrounding dwellings I observed were partly demolished and almost black in colour.

Suddenly, I looked up to a nearby hillside and was confronted by a wall of shifting eyes, extremely sad in expression. Their figures then slowly materialised, revealing a small crowd of souls wearing dirty, ill-fitting and tattered clothing. A large, menacing-looking individual then appeared and, without provocation, proceeded to scream in a hideous manner and indiscriminately rain blows on his fellow inhabitants with a huge spiked cudgel. Brother Paul must have sensed my alarm for I was instantly whisked away from this wretched place and found myself floating upwards again.

The atmosphere had now become much warmer again and I was back on the astral plane. Brother Paul, whom I now understood to have been constantly at my side throughout this chilling experience then explained to me "None of us is perfect, apart from our Heavenly Father, but those souls on one of lower planes which you have just visited have sinned much but mostly through uncontrolled anger. They will eventually earn the right to inhabit a higher plane but it will possibly be hundreds of earth years. You were never in any danger; they could not harm you. It was your spirit body which attracted them as it was a little brighter than their own." "A little brighter!", I thought to myself. This beautiful soul was kindly warning me of the dangers of allowing my lower self to take charge - of which I had been guilty the previous afternoon.

I then felt that it was time to return to my physical body and in an instant I was propelled back, entering with a noticeable shuddering jolt. I wished that I had been allowed to visit one of the higher planes but that was not on the agenda that morning. The whole experience was very informative and educational and from that particular moment I did try to consciously forgive those who had wronged me previously, as my angry thoughts were patently harmful to myself, causing the lowering of my spirit vibrations.

A week later Mrs Christine Cummings who was employed at the Hop Pole, one of our popular local Pubs, contacted me. She sounded quite distressed and explained that there had been several recent ghostly happenings in the Pub. In fact, over a number of years there had been many reports by staff of ghost sightings and apparitions. Mrs Cummings couldn't cope with the spate of poltergeist phenomena one minute longer. Foodstuffs and pans in the kitchen were being mysteriously thrown at her daily. Her daughter also worked part-time there. One day she decided to serve a chap whom she saw standing at the end of the bar and, but as she approached, he promptly disappeared, giving her an awful fright.

I prepared in the usual manner and set off to visit and investigate thoroughly. As soon as I walked into the Pub I felt the presence of a particular male spirit and could see him quite clearly. I noticed from his clothing that he had worked manually during his earth life. I asked my guides who he was and they gave me his surname, which was Thomas. They told me he worked for the Manchester Ship Canal Company in the twenties and he had died from natural causes whilst lodging nearby. He had enjoyed using this Pub, drank heavily during his earth life and was still strongly attracted to alcohol.

There was a second earthbound male spirit in the rear room. He was not very keen to come forward. I could only see his outline. He appeared cantankerous in nature and didn't want to leave either. However, I carried out the necessary procedure assisted by Brother Paul. In this case a double exorcism was needed. The restless spirits were then duly ejected and forced to gravitate to their rightful spiritual dimension. where I was sure that they would be thankful once they had eventually settled down. There have been many occasions when earthbound spirits have actually communicated with me later to thank me for their release and subsequent resettlement on being set free from their entrapment.

Time had quickly moved on and now I was battling through the winter of 1990. There seemed to be an unusual easing of spirit disturbances although I attended to a few situations requiring intervention when I was requested. During April, one particular case emerged in Longshaw Street, Warrington. The owners of the property, a young couple named Hancock, were watching television when the wall clock moved and hovered over them before dropping on to the floor. They were obviously deeply shocked and terrified following this incident.

I attended and persuaded the restless spirit of a previous tenant, who was responsible for the phenomena, to gravitate to his rightful place. Unfortunately, I had to ask for my bus fare from the couple to return home. There was never a fee considered for this very important work but it is always courteous to be offered your travelling expenses by persons you have helped. I felt a little aggrieved that my input was not properly appreciated.

In the early part of May, I was stopped in the town centre whilst on my way to pay my ground rent, by a neighbour whose friend lived in Southworth Avenue on the Bewsey council housing estate. Her pal had been experiencing much paranormal activity at her home. Not surprisingly, she was eager to move but the Housing Department initially felt that this was a ploy to move house because of her dissatisfaction with the area and stated to her that if I was brought in to investigate and confirmed a spiritual presence, they would consider the request more positively. I prepared as necessary and travelled to the house.

The presence of an earthbound spirit was confirmed to me as soon as I entered. Two people had previously lived and died in the dwelling, a father and son. They signalled through the psychic phenomena that they did not wish anyone else to live in the property. I carried out the necessary procedure and left, restoring peace, with the spirits of the father and son who were earthbound having been placed on their proper spirit realm. The Housing Department were then informed that if they needed a report from me regarding the haunting they could have one. They replied that this aspect would now be considered in the transfer request.

It was ironic really, considering the circumstances of my retirement from Warrington Borough Council for I was, to my surprise, included on a list within their Information Office as a registered psychic for general consultation.

In the late summer of 1991 I was enjoying the warmth of the August sun and watching the antics of the bumble bees collecting pollen from the honeysuckle in the rear garden when a commercial radio station from Stockport, KFM contacted me. They had obtained my telephone number from a newspaper article and asked me to appear with someone I had cured through healing to take part in a phone-in programme. I decided to ask Brenda Cornes whose recurring gynaecological problem I had previously cured. However, she couldn't make it but Mary Hart, whose back condition I had healed some time earlier, agreed to take part. We travelled to Stockport by train.

, I remember the person who was presenting the programme was Andrea, an American lady. She immediately told me that she had a back condition and that her co-presenter had a painful ankle preventing him from walking properly. She told me that they were going to put my psychic powers to the test and asked me to administer healing on the spot. She further said that she would let the listeners know of the results later. I thought that this was plainly a 'gimmick' and to be candid was not too pleased. They were both in pain and I thought "Well, if they are meant to be put right, then they will be." I didn't hesitate and agreed to participate.

Firstly I took Andrea to another room and gave her spirit healing. She then confirmed that her spinal pain had diminished. Her co-presenter then accompanied me to another room. I tended to his foot which was quite swollen. He was then able to walk normally. Andrea and I went back on air to the listeners. Andrea informed them that she and her colleague had both received healing and had been treated successfully. I continued with the phone-in. A wide range of questions were put to me by callers and I answered them without much difficulty. I knew I was being helped. At the end of the evening Mary and I returned home quite late, British Rail being to blame.

During September a well-known image consultant, Margaret Warbrick, came into my life after she consulted me requesting a psychic reading. She arrived one lunch time and as she entered the house I saw that her aura was quite colourful with a strong green tinge. She was a most refined lady and very attentive during the consultation. After I had finished the reading I remarked, "Margaret, may I tell you that you have been surrounded with the colour green since you came in." She smiled, then produced a fountain pen filled with green ink. It was indeed her favourite colour.

With the other information that had been provided for her past and present she then accepted the future pathway which was being conveyed to help her spiritual progression. She was at that time attending meditation classes under the tutorship of John Shaw who was the Director of Extra-Mural Studies at Manchester University. In his area of work he had cause to consult many psychics over the years.

Following a chat with Margaret he telephoned me and requested a psychic consultation. and though I felt sure he wanted only to check my credentials, we arranged a convenient time for the reading. During his visit some three weeks later, information that was pertinent to him flowed through, strongly and accurately. John was visibly moved because very private matters regarding his private life came to the fore. Information was being channelled through both clairaudience and clairsentience. By the time I had finished the reading, John informed me that he was fully satisfied with the clairvoyance demonstrated. I was also thankful because I was directing him for his future life tasks when he would leave his University position.

He then informed me that he wished me to attend Manchester University to give a lecture and demonstration at a weekend course which was being held in the spring of 1991. I told him that I would consider his offer and remarked to him, "It's not to provide clairvoyance if I agree to go John, I would prefer to give a demonstration of healing and to lecture on psychic matters." He accepted my terms and then informed me that I would be one of the contributors for the planned weekend University course.

Those attending would comprise physicians psychologists, lay people and students. He did ask me how I wished to be described in the course literature. I responded, "Although I am a qualified building surveyor and quantity surveyor, it would suffice for me to be described as an unorthodox Christian psychic."

I thought to myself at the time when I did give the lecture, I must impress upon the audience that the greatest psychic power came from within the Christ-force in line with natural laws which Jesus of Nazareth openly exemplified during his powerful earth mission.

CHAPTER EIGHT

Well into the spring of 1991 the invitation finally arrived from Mr Shaw for me to attend the Hollyroyde Conference Centre, Didsbury, which is part of the Manchester University network. My wife, Janet, and I travelled to Didsbury by train and I do recall that it was quite a long walk from the station and my back was giving me much discomfort. Finally, and wearily, we made it to the Centre, had a quick meal and headed straight for the lecture rooms. I had arranged this previously to cut out any waiting time.

I was met outside by the Director, John Shaw, who was obviously pleased that I had arrived, knowing that I had a problem with travelling due to my back condition. With this in mind, I asked him whether he could place a table on the platform so that I could lean against it whilst giving my presentation.. He reassured me that a table had earlier been placed there. That was extremely thoughtful of him. I then gave the lecture without notes, which I preferred, covering all aspects of the psychic field.

Both the audience and myself were getting on quite well, apart from the fact that one of my fellow contributors insisted on interrupting me, remarking, "You will not have much time left for your healing demonstration." I quickly pointed out to him that this would be taken care of by my guides. This turned out to be true. During the lecture, I tried very hard to convey spiritual truths to the people assembled because normally, it is very difficult to explain psychic truths and convey spiritual laws in a space of forty five minutes. However, I seemed to manage reasonably well.

It was then time for the healing demonstration. I had been led to believe that just a few volunteers would come forward because my time allocation was about thirty five minutes. However, as my grandfather would have said "Beghorra." Imagine my surprise when fifteen volunteers lined up to experience spiritual healing. I was also expected to provide some medical diagnosis along with the healing.

As I was doing so I came across a dental surgeon who had arranged to attend the weekend course through the help of Margaret Warbrick. He had suffered a serious leg injury some time before following a skiing accident and had travelled specifically to receive spiritual healing. He had been advised by specialists that his leg condition was so bad he was in danger of being permanently crippled. I gave him contact healing for a very short period of time, happily seeing the strength and colour of the healing rays. Subsequently I was informed that his leg condition had been cured. I must add that he actually broke down in tears, whilst I was applying the contact healing. For him it was a new spiritual experience as he admitted that he was agnostic in his religious beliefs.

Eventually I provided spiritual healing to all the volunteers who had lined up. I suddenly checked my watch. I had been so engrossed in my work I had not noticed time passing when I suddenly heard a loud voice from the back of the hall. It was the taxi driver who had arrived to collect us and clearly did not wish to be kept waiting. I winked at John who knew that I would complete the healing demonstration.

I was told later that the information about medical conditions which I had supplied, was correct and that all the volunteers had benefited from the healing which I had applied. This feedback gave me much pleasure. I had left things in the hands of Wan Chan and Red Feathers. Brother Paul had orchestrated my contribution with perfect timing.

One night, a few weeks later whilst meditating and thinking about the easing of my back condition, I was informed by the higher side that my last incarnation was four hundred years ago when I was a shaman and a bone setter, living in the northern part of South America. This revelation did not surprise me as it seemed almost uncanny that I was spending the greater part of my life carrying out spiritual work and also correcting back and neck conditions.

In the third week of May, Maria McKay and her close friend Melanie, contacted me for healing treatment. They both had troublesome physical conditions. I was able to inform Melanie that she was suffering from an ovarian cyst and I gave her healing which eventually cleared the condition. She later revisited her doctor and subsequent tests proved that a correct and early diagnosis of an ovarian cyst had been made. Mrs McKay had a serious case of womb fibroids. She had been experiencing continual bleeding and was very worried. Her doctor had suggested that she should undergo a hysterectomy. I gave her spiritual healing a few times and fortunately her problem cleared.

A researcher from Granada TV somehow got hold of my telephone number and asked me to appear on a television programme concerning psychic healing. I agreed as I thought this would be an ideal opportunity for me to promote the subject. I told the researcher that I would be accompanied by Mrs McKay and Melanie.

The night before the show was due to be broadcast a Granada employee rang Maria to confirm her previous medical condition and subsequent cure. She confirmed that the facts were accurate and also gave details of her GP's telephone number and contact address, should further verification be required. When I later attended the studios for the programme, they unfortunately did not wish me to take part in the debate as a leading subject, although I felt that the healing of Maria's condition was indeed a very strong case for discussion. According to official sources the programme ran out of time because of football coverage.

One day in the first week of September I had just arrived home with several tins of cat food for the local stray cats who were in the habit of congregating on my shed in the early morning, when one of my wife's friends, Val Barlow, rang her to say that she was a little worried about her husband, Mike, who had hurt his back and been taken into hospital after falling in the garage at his home. She said was he was in great pain. At that time he was employed as a travelling salesman and was concerned that this accident would cause him to be off work for some considerable time.

I telephoned Val later and told her that Mike was not suffering from the condition which had been diagnosed medically. The doctors had concluded that his chest cavity wall was damaged and that torn back muscles were responsible for his acute pain. Wan Chan, however, had impressed upon me that he had a disc out of place and that it could be re-housed. I immediately offered to treat him. Mike had always been sceptical but his wife persuaded him to visit me.

When he arrived I placed my fingers on a certain spot on his back and he winced in pain. Then I placed both hands on his spinal column. A thoracic joint clicked and his back began to vibrate under my hands. He then informed me that the stiffness was fading and his pain had been greatly alleviated. He did admit that he could not explain what had taken place, but was very grateful and would keep an open mind with regard to psychic matters in the future. He resumed work the following week.

The next day my wife's friend, Carol Birchall, visited the house to see Janet. I quietly remarked to Carol , "I will soon need some holy water." She replied, "It's not for me, is it?" because the week before I had been to sort out a problem at her niece's home in Delph Lane, Winwick, where a male apparition, obviously earthbound, had regularly been seen walking through the house dangling a set of keys. Subsequently, I had sorted this problem out but and she must have thought it was her house that I needed to attend to next, so I assured her that this was not the purpose for which I needed the water. I knew there was stronger work to be carried out sooner rather than later.

A further week passed and it was time for my niece's confirmation. For weeks before I had regularly been given a strong clairvoyant vision of a purple vestment, without explanation. I knew my helpers were showing this to me to prepare me for future important spiritual work.

On the Wednesday evening Janet and I took Angelina, my niece, to the church for her confirmation. A bishop from Liverpool was officiating at the service. On walking into the church, looking into the fonts I noticed that the holy water was coloured purple. I instinctively filled my water container which I had brought with me. I didn't sit down with Janet and Angelina during the service as the seating was a little low, preferring to stand at the back of the church, leaning on a conveniently placed table.

As the confirmation service ended, the Bishop walked slowly backwards up the church aisle and then to my surprise, without stopping, he seemed to be inadvertently pinning me against the table. Suddenly, it all fell into place; his purple vestments spoke volumes. I realised it would not be too long before I would be invited to alleviate a strong spiritual problem, thus confirming the reason for my previous clairvoyant visions of the vestment, provided by my guides.

At noon the next day, I received a telephone call from Catherine McManus, a journalist from the local Guardian newspaper. She asked me to go immediately to a house situated in McKee Avenue on the Longford estate in Warrington. On asking why, she replied, "There seems to be a very powerful case of a haunting and the family involved are extremely distraught. I thought you may be interested." We agreed to make further arrangements. I put the telephone down and sat quietly, asking for confirmation from the Higher side. There was a clear message that this was a genuine case and that I must deal with it. I knew that I would have to prepare thoroughly and attend to the problem.

The journalist rang again and asked me to go to the dwelling within the hour. I reminded her that, although she wanted me to go because she had arranged for a photographer to be present, it was important for me that I prepared properly beforehand. Luckily, she understood that this was necessary. I travelled to Church the following day to prepare in my normal manner. I found it closed. I knocked on the priory door and asked permission to gain access. I was met by an elderly nun who was a little reluctant to let me in. Eventually, I was allowed access and prayed for assistance for the forthcoming task.

I then arranged with the tenant of the house a convenient time for me to visit and deal with the problem she was experiencing. During the conversation the tenant informed me that although she had regularly told her husband of the various spiritual disturbances taking place, he refused to accept her version of events or that of the children. However, his opinion was soon to change as, on returning from work one evening and sitting down to this evening meal, it began to levitate from the table before crashing to the floor. He was now in no doubt and actually telephoned me himself to apologise for the further distress which was being caused by his refusal to accept his wife and children's accounts of the apparitions and phenomena.

The wife and children of this household were actually going through a harrowing time; electrical appliances were forever failing, obnoxious smells developing, apparitions were being seen accompanied by ghostly voices ordering the children to hurt each other. The atmosphere in the house was also very cold. The mother obviously couldn't cope with it much longer and in desperation had asked the parish priest to attend. He declined to and I got the impression that he had decided not to get involved.

I arranged to visit the house later in the week. I was now fully prepared. I took the holy water with me which I had collected on the evening of the confirmation. I quickly found evidence at the fireplace area in the living room that a tragic event had previously taken place, involving a young girl who had accidentally set herself on fire. Also another spirit present in the dwelling was quite malevolent, and causing many problems. The young girl who had died tragically was unhappily earthbound; the male spirit presence, who had committed suicide some years earlier. was troublesome in nature. The young girl wished for earth release; the male spirit did not, preferring to stay put and enjoy the psychological torment he was imposing.

I carried out what was necessary to release the young girl from her unhappy state and the exorcism was completed to eject the troublesome male spirit to his rightful place, amongst the spirit realms. I then blessed the house and finished with a prayer remarking to the family, "You can pray with me if you wish." They agreed. All prayer is helpful. Brother Paul had been prominent throughout the ceremony, ensuring the proper completion of the exorcism which had to be precise, as the male spirit was very stubborn and resistant.

The cold temperature immediately shifted, a very cold, strong blast of wind seemed to force its way through the house, visibly shaking the ornaments on both the sideboard and the mantelpiece. I was pleased. The task was accomplished; the family were now at peace; the young child had been taken to her proper realm; the troublesome male spirit exorcised and taken to his rightful spiritual dimension where he would receive the rehabilitation required.

A month later, in the final week of October 1991 I underwent a strong spiritual experience myself which was orchestrated to test my character. My own circle of helpers were not involved on this occasion. I had always told my friends about the necessity of being charitable to those around us, being of the opinion that we should give freely, even to those we suspected of being dishonest, because any negative reflection was to be on them not the provider. One Thursday evening I was to be put to the test.

I strolled off to the Ring O'Bells Public House which was not far from my home. I usually never took more than a couple of quid with me as I never consumed much beer. Often when I wanted to be alone I could be found in the back room, quietly reading. Although there were other times when I enjoyed the company of friends and there would be lively discussions about rugby, politics and current events. On this particular evening, I felt the need, unusually for me, to take eight pounds with me to the Pub. This sum was what I had left to last me personally for the week.

As I was making my way to the Pub, I glanced to my left and there was an elderly chap sitting in a hunched position on a nearby bench. Surprisingly, he had pulled his coat over his head and appeared to be asleep. As the evening wore on I decided to leave the Pub early on my own. This was most unusual for me, as I used to walk home with two friends whose company I was in the habit of sharing on this particular night. As this was a Thursday evening the Pub was very busy.

The streets were unusually quiet as I walked past the bench I had passed earlier and noticed the elderly chap was still sitting there. This time his coat was pulled down to reveal an unshaven and haggard face. He was not drunk, however, and as I walked past, I heard him speak to me, "You are the one I want, I knew you would return. Please give me a minute of your time." I must admit I was a little wary but I didn't hesitate and walked back. As I got close to him he stood up and asked me for instructions on how to get to the local Salvation Army hostel.

As it happened I directed him to the wrong building which was the Citadel. It didn't really matter. Without thinking about it, I put my hand in my pocket and gave him the eight pounds. The other two lads I had spent the evening with had bought the drinks as I had bought them the previous week, so I still had the money in my pocket. I told him, "Go and get yourself a cup of tea and a hot meal. This will be enough I feel sure." He then broke down in tears, "I'm not a beggar." I insisted, "You must take it." He wrapped his arms around me, hugged me and sat down again. I bade him goodnight and began to make my way home.

I had walked about a hundred yards when it was impressed on my mind that this was not a normal person that I had just encountered, but a higher spirit entity. The spirit world had arranged for my charitable credentials in respect of my fellow human beings to be examined to a greater degree.

Three months later I thought I had spotted the same man whilst making my way to the bus station in the town centre on a deserted Sunday morning. I went over to him and our eyes locked in recognition. I immediately commented, "Can you kindly tell me where the Salvation Army hostel is?" he stood and pointed in the wrong direction. I knew this wrong advice was deliberate and offered him a small sum of money to let him know I was aware of the situation. "Thanks very much," he said after I gave him the money, "you have helped me a great deal. You know, you are a real gentleman." It was the same spirit entity I had met previously outside the Ring O'Bells Public House. I walked away without looking back.

From that moment on I developed much stronger mediumistically. I was seeing people's auras even more clearly; my intuition was also getting stronger and my psychic senses were now far more acute.

I frequently had welcome distractions from my spiritual and psychic activities through the regular vociferous demands of the stray cats who descended on my yard, morning and evening, for their meals. Our own pet cat Suzie seemed permanently involved in skirmishes with them. However, they always provided Janet and myself with much pleasure and responded with great affection.

We enjoyed a quiet autumn and Christmas. Early in the following year, 1992, as I scanned my roof for storm damage my telephone rang. I answered and heard a distinctive north-eastern accent, "Hello, Mr McGrath your name and telephone number has been forwarded to me by one of my charity helpers with regard to you possibly helping me out with a long standing leg injury." I replied, "I am prepared to do my best, as always." It quickly transpired that he was an international footballer who was playing for a leading northern premiership team at the time and, for obvious reasons, wished to be treated discreetly. We arranged a time for him to pop down the following week.

On his arrival at my home, I found him to be polite, confident and quite modest. His injury, an internal haemorrhage of the ankle, was not responding to club treatment and his team doctor wished him to finish for the season to allow complete rest in order to cure the injury. He, however, was desperate to continue playing and be involved in the crucial final games which would decide the outcome of the championship. As he had previously received spiritual healing with positive results he was prepared to try this form of therapy once more. I administered spiritual healing on three more occasions. Happily, he did recover sufficiently to take part in the critical final games of the season and the healing applied was undoubtedly worthwhile.

I did however, have a difficult time with the local boys in the neighbourhood who, being very keen soccer fans, easily recognised my footballer guest and his personalised car number plate when he arrived for his healing sessions and enthusiastically descended upon me each time he left, brushing away my denials and asking the most unlikely personal questions as to his likes and dislikes. I myself was simply pleased to have helped with relieving his on-going discomfort.

During the next three months I cut down on my spiritual work in order to rest my back for longer periods of time, as it was deteriorating considerably. We also had the house fully carpeted which pleased Janet immensely.

In the month of August that year, Chancellor's Estate Agents of Warrington presented me with the opportunity to carry out a pleasing soul rescue. A year earlier a medium had informed the staff that there were demonic forces within the premises responsible for causing a sequence of bad luck to anybody who entered a particular upstairs room. There had been a good deal of spiritual disturbance on these premises for several years. Apparitions were seen quite regularly; clocks stopped frequently accompanied by many other kinds of poltergeist phenomena being reported. The manager rang me and asked me to investigate. I agreed to visit the building to clear up the problem. It had been conveyed to me clairvoyantly that the source of the problem was an earthbound spirit seeking help, hence the paranormal activity and not a demonic force as previously reported.

I arranged an appropriate time with the manager for my visit and prepared in my usual manner. When I arrived at the building I was immediately directed towards one of the female staff. Her aura was quite fiery; she was giving off much uncontrolled energy and was psychically a very sensitive girl, inadvertently acting as a beacon for the earthbound spirit seeking help. She was the reason why this particular spirit had gone into this building.

The presence was the spirit of a young girl. I could sense her everywhere. Above all she needed desperately to be removed from her earthbound state. I then located her. She had actually been in the spirit state for the best part of two hundred years but had always been afraid to move through the astral gate. I felt a sharp stomach ache and then it was explained to me by Brother Paul that she had died with gastroenteritis at quite a young age. She beckoned to me suggesting that she wanted help. I asked her guardian spirit for the gentlest assistance for the trapped child spirit to be taken to her rightful place. This was effected and she was met immediately by her loved ones in spirit. I was very pleased as it had been so gentle. I blessed the premises and informed the staff about the spiritual activity which had taken place.

It was then that the manager told me, "Two newspaper reporters have arrived - I had told them that you would be conducting an exorcism." I remarked to her that I hadn't asked for them to be present and was pleased that I had actually finished my work before their arrival. On meeting them I explained that it wasn't an exorcism as such, but a soul rescue, which had been carried out. I left the building quickly, mission accomplished, the young soul finally reunited with her loved ones.

CHAPTER NINE

It was a warm and humid day in July when I rang Janet at her office. She was now employed at Warrington Hospital as a PA in the Administration Department. She had forgotten her lunch and I offered to take it in to her. On arrival I gave two of her girl colleagues their numeroscopes which they had previously requested.

Instinctively, I felt drawn to an empty seat which belonged to Russell Hamilton, one of the Administration Managers. Promptly I received a message from the higher side that I should leave him some pertinent advice in a brief note warning him about his future health should he continue to neglect his body's nutritional requirements. This was left on his desk. I then made my way home, hoping he would heed my warning.

My mother was now getting on in years. Aged 81, she was now far less mobile yet still very alert, her mental faculties still very sharp. I enjoyed the weekly visits to see her. She never failed to surprise me, often presenting us with little gadgets for our kitchen which she had purchased for Janet from the local market. I knew that my father was frequently around her but never touched on the subject as it made her feel a little uncomfortable.

Approaching the August Bank Holiday, one morning I found I was drifting away in a light trance when the familiar voice of Brother Paul spoke to me quietly, "Please prepare, you have important work in store!" I prepared in my usual manner and five days later I was contacted by Mr Denton , a local building contractor based in the Woolston district of Warrington. He had unsuccessfully tried to reach me through Frank Hutson but eventually obtained my telephone number from the press, following their coverage of one of the soul rescues in which I had been involved. He asked nervously, "Mr McGrath, I have read about your psychic work. Would you please help my wife and I? We are desperate."

The outline of their problem then emerged. Their daughter, aged sixteen, was proving very difficult, not in the normal way with teenage problems of boyfriends etc. but being at the core of some very strong paranormal activity, which included constant foul smells pervading the dwelling and spirit voices being heard incessantly. This was confirmed by my guides who informed me clairvoyantly that ouija-board activity carried out previously in their bungalow had allowed certain inferior and confused spirits to intrude upon the young girl and also to take residence in the family home.

I then arranged to quickly visit the dwelling as I had already prepared myself following the earlier messages from my guides. Mr Denton picked me up in his truck the next day. I instinctively asked him if the problem had worsened. It had, following the contact by telephone complete pandemonium had broken loose. The electrical power circuits had blown; a serious burst on the water supply occurred and a constant rattling noise was heard, which was worsening by the hour.

As soon as I arrived I headed for the living room where I had asked their daughter to wait for me. Walking through the hallway I was confronted by a large male spirit form glaring menacingly at me . I focused upon him, quietly conveying my intentions to remove him. My guides then materialised strongly. This particular spirit then retreated. The other earthbound spirit was female and appeared in the kitchen area. I communicated to her in my thoughts and discovered that, because of marital problems, she had previously committed suicide and was, consequently, lost in the grey zones and had inadvertently entered the dwelling, being drawn through the ouija-board session that had taken place. I explained to Mr and Mrs Denton what was to happen and then commenced with the soul rescue of the earthbound female spirit.

On completion I turned my attention to the daughter who was sitting on a couch. Our eyes engaged. Her eyes were not young, bright and friendly but old, stark and bloodshot. The male earthbound spirit I had first encountered was now possessing her once again as he had done for the best part of twelve months causing her strange behaviour which had resulted in her being medically examined on three occasions for possible psychological disturbance.

The necessary exorcism was conducted and I saw him being escorted through the astral doorway by my guides. The daughter immediately relaxed and the atmosphere changed. Brother Paul confirmed to me, "Kevin, God's wishes have been carried out!" I then left, preferring to catch a bus back as my back was still protesting fiercely from the truck ride!

One evening later that month, after a prolonged discussion Janet and I decided to have a night out in the Lion Public House on the Saturday of the August Bank Holiday weekend. We found it uncomfortable, packed and very noisy but decided to stay for a short time. Later Christine Cummings and her husband Paul popped in, spotted us and immediately came over to our table.

Before I had time to enter in a little banter with them, Wan Chan comunicated to me quite clearly above the noise that was booming throughout the Pub, "Christine has a serious gynaecological problem. Please advise Paul to cancel the package holiday to Greece which he has recently arranged as she will be taken into hospital unexpectedly quite soon to be treated." I then asked Christine if she had been feeling a little off colour. She replied, "Well, as a matter of fact, I have been suffering spasmodic pains in my groin for the past week. It's probably something I have eaten." I turned to Paul and advised him to cancel the holiday which was due in a fortnight and to recover his deposit. I then explained to Christine what information I had just received from my guide. They both agreed to consider my message.

Paul contacted me five days later to inform me that Christine had been admitted to hospital with the medical problem which had been conveyed to me earlier by Wan Chan. The decision to cancel the holiday had been made for them by the hand of fate. This experience had proved most informative. Most authors of spiritual books which I had read stated that to clearly receive good information clairvoyantly there should always be a peaceful atmosphere beforehand. I was now aware that they were not strictly accurate in their theories.

During September 1992 Sandra Allen, a practising hypnotherapist from Northwich, whom I knew well, referred to me a leading acupuncturist from the Manchester area. She was suffering from a painful back condition, for which she had sought treatment from a local osteopath who had been treating her for several months, but to little effect. A convenient time was arranged for her to visit me.

On arrival she was obviously in much pain. Her back problem was immediately shown to me clairvoyantly by my helpers from the higher side. It transpired that one of the facet joints in her thoracic region was displaced and also a lumbar disc was pressing on a root nerve. It was then conveyed to me clairaudiently to ask her to lie in a certain position. I then administered spiritual healing. There were two loud clicks; I was then informed by Red Feathers, "The problem is now solved, but you must apply more healing to alleviate the inflammation." This was carried out. The lady got up quickly, with a look of amazement on her face. Her back pain had gone and her condition was now cured. She admitted to me that she was intrigued because, as a professional practitioner in complementary therapy, she usually spent at least an hour to treat patients. Yet, within five minutes, her condition had been healed. She left, thanking me profusely.

Sandra Allen rang me the following day and reported that she had been contacted by the acupuncturist who was still a little perplexed by what had happened. However, she did remark, that should she be troubled again she would not hesitate to contact me. My efforts had been worthwhile in opening her mind to the possibilities of spiritual intercession.

On the final day of September during the early evening I was lying on the living room floor. My wife often jokingly referred to me as a lazy old English sheep dog because of the time I spent lying near the fire. I slowly began meditating. Janet was sitting on the couch watching 'Coronation Street' on the television. 'Soap operas' provided her with a welcome escape, as her job at the local hospital was very demanding.

Suddenly a spirit hand began to clutch my hand. The hand

was quite bulbous (and being a palmist I knew that if the Mount of Venus, the area surrounding the thumb was puffy and raised, it indicated great love) and ice-cold, causing me to shiver from head to toe. It was clutching me very firmly then, as I quickly acknowledged the gesture, the hand released its grip and faded. I knew that when one touches those in spiritual form the physical sensation is usually one of extreme cold or heat. For me the feeling was of extreme cold.

On reflection I realised I was cheekily being reminded by my guides that my left hand was the hand where the healing powers were being directed. Red Feathers later confirmed this to me. The healing energies are always channelled within the laws of polarity. This was a splendid experience of spiritual physical contact. I turned towards to Janet and explained to her what had happened. Although somewhat surprised, she didn't dispute my account. In the past I had seen my guides but this was the first time I had experienced such strong physical contact from the higher side.

Two weeks later Karen Bentley, a hair stylist and an old friend from Lymm, Cheshire, wrote to me asking me to help one of her clients, Pat Simpson, who lived in Stockport near Manchester. Pat had suffered from multiple sclerosis for a number of years and her condition was deteriorating, causing her to become deeply depressed. Her husband Alan, was extremely worried about her state of mind and her frequent hints about committing suicide as the depression was taking a deeper hold. I replied quickly to Mrs Simons, arranging a time for her to visit me to receive spiritual healing.

After writing the letter, I sat quietly and asked my guides if a cure could be effected for Pat. Wan Chan spoke to me in his usual slow and sure manner, "Kevin you will channel the healing rays for this lady, not to cure her condition, as her karmic pattern does not allow for a cure but she is in much mental despair and enough of the divine source will be directed to arrest and alleviate her illness so that she will be much happier in mind and better equipped to accept her restrictions!"

Mrs Simpson arrived three days later with her husband, Alan. I gave her the first of several healing treatments and, as Wan Chan had previously stated, Pat began to improve and her depression lifted. Even though she was still inconvenienced by certain limitations which the multiple sclerosis caused, the spiritual healing sessions had obviously rejuvenated her. The experience was also a vital lesson personally, reminding me that not all disease can be cured by the healer, no matter how much he or she may wish for success. The truth is that healing intercessions are completely governed by natural laws, implemented by the spirit guides who work through the chosen earth instrument.

It was now Monday of the fourth week of October and I was consulted by Mr and Mrs Pritchard who lived in Southworth Lane, Winwick, near Warrington. Their house, which was about one hundred and fifty years old had been converted from an old farm building. Mrs Pritchard spoke to me in frightened tones of the paranormal activity that had regularly been taking place in the dwelling. It transpires that there had been three previous owners who had moved, owing to a succession of ghost sightings and regular poltergeist phenomena.

Whilst arranging a time for me to investigate the house it was conveyed to me by Brother Paul that the problems were being caused by an earthbound spirit in the form of the first house owner, a lady who had been the matron of a psychiatric hospital. The psychic phenomena included the regular appearance of many strange and heavy insect infestations. The couple had been warned before they purchased the house by a friend who lived nearby. He had been told by the previous owners of a female apparition forming whilst the family were having lunch, which spoke out vociferously, ordering them to leave the house immediately. In fact it had been this final incident which had forced them to sell the property.

Before requesting my intercession Mrs Pritchard had already invited the local vicar from the local Winwick church to resolve the haunting problem. He tried but his attempts had actually made the situation worse. Three days later I arrived at the house and as I entered, felt much animosity from the discarnate female spirit. Instinctively, I searched for the rear living-room where I knew she was located. She had spent most of her time in this room during her earth life. I immediately saw her spirit form hurtle towards me and just as quickly saw a wave of Brother Paul's arm which seemed to knock her backwards. She had been aiming to breach my aura which, fortunately, had been protected with my customary psychic preparation.

She seemed to be preparing to launch another assault against me, when I began to effect the exorcism necessary to move her from her earthbound state. I saw that she was surrounded by a shower of colours as Brother Paul, with other helpers from her own soul group, took her upwards through the gate of light on the astral plane. Almost immediately a feeling of tranquillity prevailed. My guide confirmed that she had now been permanently removed from the dwelling and that peace had been restored. I then informed Mrs Pritchard what I had done, left the house and later thanked my spirit guides for their great assistance which enabled me to carry out the necessary exorcism.

It was a Tuesday evening in the second week of December, Janet and I were organising a Christmas gift list when the telephone rang. A softly spoken Asian lady named Meena Rajdev asked, "Kevin McGrath, is that you? I am from London; your telephone number has been given to me by a friend whom you helped some years ago. Please can you help my brother Kisha!" She explained that he was seriously ill in a London hospital following major heart surgery. The doctors had informed his family that they did not expect him to survive, as everything possible had been done medically. I heard confirmation from my guides that I should administer distant spirit healing and that he would recover. I then conveyed this information to Meena.

Two days elapsed before she rang me again. This time there was a joyful tone to her voice, "Kevin, my brother has recovered rapidly, to the amazement of the hospital staff. Thank you so much." I felt privileged to have been instrumental in this strong spiritual intercession.

As I was closing our conversation a voice from the higher side quickly broke in and stated, "I am Meena's mother. I have been aware of her recent grieving for me, whilst my son was seriously ill. Please tell her I am not dead but very much alive and with my sister who passed before me. I am with Meena often, giving comfort and strength." To substantiate this she continued to provide me with further details of her maiden name, favourite clothes, flowers and other personal information concerning the family. I again conveyed this to Meena, who became very emotional, commenting, "How did you know her maiden name and these other facts?"

As a Hindu she was not familiar with the workings of spirit. She was, nonetheless, reassured but still remained unconvinced as to the existence of her mother's sister as she had been led to believe that her mother did not have a sister. The next day, after contacting her father, this fact was confirmed. The sister had died very young following an illness but because of a complicated family rift, this information was withheld from Meena. She would now cease to grieve for her mother and thanked me again.

I felt very pleased for Meena and her family and also acknowledged the fact that God works in his own mysterious ways, breaching the divide between different religious barriers in his own perfect manner, within spiritual laws that embraced all souls. Meena was to contact me again for help when her baby niece underwent surgery and as a consequence became seriously ill. Once again, the bright spirit guides interceded through spiritual healing, restoring her to perfect health although it was not expected by the medics. Meena's faith in God's natural universal law was now more concrete than ever.

The start of January of 1993 saw the beginning of a very cold spell and I keenly waited for spring to arrive. During this time a Catholic priest from Birmingham contacted me asking for help with a serious eye condition. He had obtained my number from the Psychic News and having read about my healing work he genuinely believed that I could help him which I found most refreshing. He said that he felt that he had been directed to me for help. He also explained that he, too, was psychically sensitive and he added, "I carry out my church duties to the letter but I realise there is great truth in spiritual healing." We both spoke about the magic of psychic healing and I remarked to him, "The greatest psychic healer to grace the earth was Jesus Christ." We both agreed on that point. I mentioned that St Paul in the chapter of the Corinthians, had stated that those born with spiritual gifts had a duty to use them.

He seemed most concerned about his eye problems. I then explained that I would send absent healing, asking my guides to help him as much as possible. He later told me that his eyes had improved very much and, periodically to this day, he still rings me for a chat. I had already reassured him that I would never reveal his identity as his Bishop would not hesitate to have him thrown out of the priesthood, which was a sad reflection on the church's stance on spirit healing but, nonetheless, was the case.

The spring had now arrived and I felt somewhat relieved as the winter damp and cold always aggravated my back problems. During the latter part of May, Reg Fitzpatrick, a Liverpudlian spiritualist referred a lady work colleague, Mrs Helen Jacobs, for me to help her with an illness which was causing chronic nausea and general malaise.

Two weeks later she arrived at my house. I informed her that in the course of the consultation it might be possible for me to use the information conveyed that was possibly channelled through clairvoyance, during the healing session. She said rather flippantly, "Really! This is a procedure which I find hard to accept." Although we all have a duty to love our fellow souls, it is not at all unusual for one to take a dislike to a person. Obviously she was proving very unco-operative. Mrs Jacobs continued in a most ungracious manner, "I have come here to listen but not necessarily to follow your advice. Reg was insistent that I came and in the circumstances I did not wish to refuse and hurt his feelings!" I noticed that her aura was three parts red and brown, usually indicating aggression and negativity. Undoubtedly she would prove to be a difficult patient.

Nevertheless, I proceeded. Information was sent to me that her problem was due mainly to a high cholesterol count. Fatty tissues had formed around her kidneys causing a blood disorder which, in turn, caused the chronic symptoms. The natural remedy, which was supplied clairvoyantly, was spiritual healing and certain supplements were to be taken alongside a change in diet. I passed on this information to her. She refused the spiritual healing and said that she would not use the supplements unless advised by a medical specialist. She was due to see a specialist for examination and tests and I felt that she would only respect his recognition of my assessment and advice.

Two months later Reg rang to inform me that the lady had undergone a full medical examination and exhaustive tests. She had revealed to him that the diagnosis I had provided proved to be accurate, also that she had informed the specialist of her visit to me and recounted what I had stated about her condition, upon which he had remarked, "If that is the case, I suggest you take the supplements recommended - I would in similar circumstances!" His other advice was for her to adopt a special diet, exactly the same advice my guide had offered initially. I also felt the earlier application of healing would have made much difference. She was patently sent to test my patience and further my understanding of fellow souls.

Saturday, 20th March, the day before Mother's Day was unforgettable, regrettably, for the saddest of reasons. Several bombs planted by terrorists in a crowded part of Bridge Street in the heart of Warrington town centre exploded without warning, causing the tragic deaths of two young boys, Jonathan Ball and Tim Parry. Many horrific injuries were suffered by other innocent shoppers caught in the blast. I prayed long and hard for the families of the bereaved and injured. I knew that those souls responsible for the outrage would ultimately face appropriate judgement through the process of God's natural laws that are continually implemented on the higher side of life.

On the second Monday in May, Janet rang me from work to inform me that Russell Hamilton, senior hospital manager had been rushed into his local hospital, seriously ill, his condition diagnosed as Guillan-Barre syndrome, caused by a lowering of the immune system. Immediately, my mind raced back to the previous year when I had warned him, in writing, to slow down on his workload or he would fall ill sooner rather than later, also adding that it would be a virus infection causing the eventual illness. I asked for healing assistance to be conveyed from the higher side for his recovery and waited. Three days later I was informed by my spirit guides that Russell's illness had now been attended to and that he would eventually pull through.

Later in the spring of 1994 Russell was back at his desk and fully recovered when he confirmed that in the acute stages of his illness, whilst in intensive care and fully conscious, he underwent a strong spiritual experience, actually being aware of my guides attending to him. He admitted that he was no longer sceptical about discarnate spirit entities and the existence of a spirit world, for him they now warranted further consideration.

CHAPTER TEN

As I got home from the local pharmacy on a glorious day in July, 1993, with a three months supply of dihydrocodeine painkillers, the telephone rang. Mr and Mrs Ollerenshaw of Cliftonville Road, Woolston near Warrington, requested my help with regard to a haunting problem. They owned a large German shepherd dog which, for no accountable reason, was howling incessantly day and night and would not move from the corner of the living room. They had also been woken up by shrieks of laughter during the night with no apparent logical explanation. I was alerted by my guides that one female earthbound spirit was causing the problems and had been in the house for some time, causing the rapid turnover of owners, a fact the couple were unaware of. I arranged a convenient time to pop down during the following week.

The next day Mr Ollerenshaw contacted me by telephone to tell me that they had walked into the living room that morning to be greeted by a large scribbled message on the wall which clearly announced, "KEEP OUT!" It was not possible for anyone to have entered the house that night as it was electronically alarmed; this phenomenon only served to frighten them further. The earthbound spirit was directing her advice to me. She knew of my intentions and was most displeased.

A week later, after preparing in my usual way, I entered the dwelling and greeted Mr and Mrs Ollerenshaw. The psychic energy encountered was found to be quite strong. Slowly, the spirit form of an old lady materialised in the kitchen area, staring directly at me, the howling of the dog reaching a crescendo at this time, obviously aware of her presence. I conveyed a quick message to her that she would finally have to leave. This was followed by an instant rush of cold air around my aura as she moved forward and clinically attempted to breach it, which would have disturbed my consciousness considerably. With the help of my guides the necessary exorcism was then conducted quickly and thoroughly. I saw her being escorted firmly by radiant spirit figures who were taking her through the astral gateway to her rightful spirit dimension.

At once the dog sprang up from the corner and rapidly began licking each one of us in turn, its tail wagging furiously. The atmosphere had now also changed noticeably for the better. I explained to Mr and Mrs Ollerenshaw what had taken place and left satisfied that peace had been fully restored. Finding the bus stop I sat on a comfortable wooden bench and thanked my guides for their assistance. The heat of the sun's rays seemed to penetrate my whole being whilst I waited for my bus to return home.

In the third week of September, Kathleen Bradshaw of Riversdale, Martinscroft, requested me to provide her with a psychic reading. During the reading I informed her that her husband was very depressed and for the betterment of his health, needed to be restored to employment after being made redundant two years earlier. Other relevant factors emerged concerning her own circumstances, one particular warning indicated a future kidney problem which did materialise later and at the time given. However, the chief issue which was being impressed upon me was to provide Mrs Bradshaw with a definite indication of future employment which was of extreme importance to them both.

I was provided, as I thought, with the actual beginning of the 1994 new year for this job opportunity to arise and conveyed it accordingly. A few minutes after she had left the house the unmistakable vibrations and mischievous tones of Wan Chan impinged upon my consciousness, "Typical Irishman Kevin, please contact Mrs Bradshaw quickly and correct the message you have just relayed. Not on January first in your western New Year for the new job placement but February tenth, the date of the beginning of my Chinese New Year!" With some difficulty I obtained her telephone number and put matters right.

I learned later that Mr Bradshaw was offered a job, unexpectedly, and commenced work on February tenth 1994. Wan Chan had been incredibly accurate and his droll sense of humour had been a source of amusement and a typical reflection of his advanced spirit's individuality.

Throughout my psychic development there had only been infrequent occasions when my services had been called upon to locate missing persons. One particular experience I recall quite clearly. During the third week of July Margaret Gibbs, a local girl whose friend had earlier consulted me for a psychic reading, rang me very early one morning requesting my assistance.

She was most distraught as her mother had been missing from home for seven days, without apparent reason and press appeals concerning her disappearance had drawn a blank. The police suspected that she had wandered off and possibly committed suicide in a depressed frame of mind. To this effect they dragged the River Mersey, a local reservoir and the Manchester Ship Canal in an attempt to find her body. Their efforts proved unsuccessful. I assured Margaret that I would do my level best to seek as much information as possible through clairvoyance, to assist in locating her mother.

Immediately, whilst still holding the telephone in my hand, my guides spoke to me: "Kevin, the missing lady is still alive and well, although somewhat confused. She is to be found some distance away from her home, within a self-contained residence. She has also taken enough money with her to provide for her daily needs." I quickly passed this information to Margaret which gave her great relief. Three days later the police tracked her down to a caravan in Wales and she was subsequently reunited with her family.

In the early part of September, Margaret contacted me again, apologising profusely for not contacting me at the time of her mother's return. I reassured her that her apology was not important as I felt pleased and privileged to have been the channel for the crucial and comforting information which had been provided to her initially in her desperate hour of need. This episode was a strong confirmation that the higher side will always release the necessary information in these circumstances, through a psychic instrument, if it suits God's plans for the individuals concerned.

The third week of October, 1993, had elapsed and I had finally finished a two month course of physiotherapy, involving ultrasound and interferential treatment for my lower back and sciatica problems. Alas, I had not gained much pain relief but I felt obliged to give this mode of therapy another try.

The higher side must have been closely in tune with my concentration on my spinal column, for the following summer of 1994 was chiefly concerned with the provision of spiritual healing for a number of back and neck conditions, chronic and acute, all addressed in a different manner and each surprisingly, remedied following a single application of healing. This was quite a significant development for there had been many occasions when I was unable to improve conditions as quickly as I desired.

The people I was able to help were:

December 1993, Paul Smythe, a local builder who had been incapacitated for three years because of a slipped lumbar disc; all previous medical treatments had failed. One treatment and then cured.

January 1994, Brenda Cornes, a hospital nurse in Warrington who had a slipped disc of two years standing. One treatment and cured.

March 1994, Janet Monaghan, a hospital sister in Warrington, suffered two slipped discs for four years and different treatments had been unsuccessful. One treatment then cured. Her mother and father, both suffering from spinal problems for a number of years received healing and were subsequently cured.

May 1994, Nonie Small of Locking stumps, a housewife suffering three slipped discs and displaced vertebrae for a period of five years received spiritual healing and was cured after one treatment.

It did seem a very compressed period of healing for back conditions and when I asked my guides why this was so, they informed that as I was suffering an acute period of discomfort myself, I would prove to be a much better and compassionate instrument for those souls engineered into my path to be treated.

During the final week of July 1994, the last person who consulted me during this period was Terry Butler, a professional musician who had a serious neck condition for four years and was cured. He also referred his wife Linda for attention. She had ruptured wrist tendons and I gave her spiritual healing which I knew was quite strong. The next day her arm was nearly back to normal. Linda was emotionally moved by this experience and admitted that her non-belief in alternative healing therapies was to be reviewed.

The summer of 1994 was now slipping away, the evenings were slowly becoming a little colder and once again the dreaded winter approached. In late September, Mrs Jacqueline Bell of Thelwall, Cheshire, contacted me following a press article featuring my spiritual healing work. She had suffered from acne rosacae quite badly for a period of eight years and had undergone every known treatment through three separate dermatologists without a grain of success. I was her last hope of relief from her condition.

As she entered my house I noticed how badly affected her face was as a result of the acne and as she sat down Wan Chan informed me that her condition was due to dietary deficiencies following the birth of her child eight years before. A list of supplements were subsequently provided to me, which would correct the problem along with a brief application of spiritual healing. I advised her that it would take a month for the supplements and healing to take effect. She replied, "I am prepared to wait six months for any improvement which would allow me to relax and to socialise freely again!" I also needed to apply some more spiritual healing two weeks later, a request with which Mrs Bell agreed.

A fortnight elapsed and she arrived at my house for the second healing treatment. As I opened the door she met me with a huge smile and an almost clear complexion and commented, "The acne has nearly gone, I'm so pleased and really flabbergasted by it all!" I reassured her that her face would now remain normal. With that she squeezed my hands very firmly, thanked me again and left still smiling broadly. I, in turn, thanked my guides for their intercession; the condition was not life-threatening but for Mrs Bell the cure was of special importance and I felt sure that the experience had touched her soul.

The rugby league season was now in full swing and I had great expectations of the Warrington team's success. Rugby was always an extra welcome diversion along with my care of the local stray cats.

Sometime in the final days of September, I received a telephone call from Mr Stevens-Pickett who resided in Eastchurch, Sheerness, Kent. He had obtained my number from the Psychic News and was desperately seeking help following nine months of constant pain with a broken rib, caused by a heavy fall whilst working on his small-holding. He informed me that the medical opinion was that no further help could be given to ease his pain. Private osteopathic treatment had helped a little but now his discomfort was as bad as ever. I reassured him that I would ask for the strongest possible healing intercession, especially as he was solely responsible for the care of his goats and sheep which he regarded as special friends. He was clearly a man who shared my love of animals.

Two days later, in the early hours, whilst awaking from a light sleep, Red Feathers appeared and informed me, "Kevin, both Wan Chan and I have attended to the kind soul from Kent, a rib cartilage under the fourth rib, which the doctors had not discovered, was found to be displaced, I have pushed it back into its normal position and the healing rays have been applied in force. He is now fine!" I fell back into sleep knowing that Mr Stevens-Pickett would now be pain-free and felt pleased for him and also relieved that his animals would be cared for properly.

Two weeks later I was in the process of dealing with a council tax payment reminder when Mr Stevens-Pickett rang. His voice was anxious in tone yet I sensed his relief, "Mr McGrath, I cannot thank you enough, my condition has been cured, the pain has gone completely." I then informed him of his rib cartilage displacement and the subsequent spirit healing intercession. He then recounted how on the night of the rib condition being cured by my guides, he had woken up in the early hours experiencing a very sharp pain in the region of his fourth rib which intrigued him as it was his eighth rib which had been broken previously.

The next morning for the first time in ten months, he was free of pain and back to full mobility. I thanked my helpers for their kind works. The message immediately flashed back, "It is now possible for us to carry out stronger work through you Kevin, what is commonly known on the earth plane as psychic surgery. Other deserving souls will be engineered to contact you - be ready!"

The Christmas period of 1994 was now looming rapidly and colder winds were prevailing, much to my displeasure.

The telephone rang very early one morning in early December, "Hello, my name is Pat and I am the manager of 'Quincy's', a well-known hotel in Northwich Cheshire. We have a serious haunting problem. Your telephone number has been passed onto us by one of your fellow psychics. Can you help?" She continued, telling me of a range of inexplicable occurrences at the hotel which had happened during the previous year. The staff and guests felt that they were in the middle of an 'Amityville' style horror experience. I then comforted her with a reassurance that I would go and visit the hotel and carry out the necessary follow-up spiritual procedures. I asked Brother Paul for further confirmation of the events described by Pat. He quietly replied, "Three tasks to be carried out at this building, and soon, so peace may be granted for those in the flesh and those in spiritual limbo!"

A time was agreed with Pat, who would pick me up and take me to the hotel on the outskirts of Northwich. This duly happened five days later after I had prepared myself earlier with my usual ritual of aura protection and meditation. On walking through the hotel foyer I was met by a procession of spirit children who danced gleefully past me and stepped down a flight of stairs leading to the ground floor bedrooms. There were thirty two rooms in the hotel. The spirit children quickly dematerialised apart from one confused looking child with long hair in ringlets. My guides quickly informed me that this child had tragically drowned quite a long time earlier in a nearby pond and was, unfortunately, earthbound.

They also said that two male earthbound spirits were present on the premises having been attracted by the movements of the other discarnate spirits. Obviously they derived much pleasure in tormenting the female staff. I then asked Pat, who was walking slowly behind me, whether there had been any male apparitions sighted. She confirmed that there had been several sightings. I then felt that I had to move into the main bar. As I approached the counter I saw the spirit figures of two males, both dressed in farm labourers' clothing. They fastened onto my gaze and registered their disapproval of my presence. I then quietly communicated with them to inform them that they would soon be placed on their rightful spiritual plane. Brother Paul quickly reminded me, "Please commence with the young child spirit first. These two restless souls will not be moving anywhere!"

The full necessary spiritual procedures were then carried out. The spirit children who had been attracted to the cries of the girl spirit locked on the earth plane were gently escorted back to their spirit home. The earthbound spirit of the child was also escorted very carefully through the astral gate, to be met by her family links in a spirit dimension where they had been waiting for their transition. Finally the exorcism of the two troublesome male spirits was swiftly carried out.

Afterwards I conducted a full holy water blessing of the entire hotel. The staff and long term guests were then informed of the spiritual works that had been carried out and they sighed with relief, saying that they were at the end of their tether. Pat gave me a lift back home. Halfway through the car journey her father slowly materialised at her side. I quickly told her of his presence and described him as clearly as possible. She replied, "Yes, your description is accurate, it must be him. He died some years ago. It does give much comfort to know that he lives on." Little did she know that he had been chiefly instrumental in pushing her to have the haunting problem addressed and was pleased for her and the folk at the hotel that peace had now been restored. 'Quincy's' was back to normal.

I was quietly pleased to have negotiated the Christmas period. It was far too commercial, the holy event of the Christ's birth seemed to have little significance to most people, yet it did provide Janet with some much needed rest from her very taxing job at the local hospital.

On a very cold evening in late January of the new year, Louise McKinnon visited me with a severe shoulder problem. Louise was staying with relatives, having flown in from Australia for a holiday and also to seek a cure for her shoulder injury that had puzzled the medics and the alternative therapists back in Australia. She was unable to lift her arm above chest height and her torso was twisted following an accident that had happened some time previously. My guides informed me that the medical diagnosis offered to Louise in Australia was incorrect. Indeed, her problem was simply due to certain shoulder nerves being trapped and that the condition would be quickly sorted out.

I proceeded to give her healing; my fingers were drawn across her shoulder blades; her back suddenly straightened out under my hand. I asked Louise to lift her arm, which she did freely. Her eyes sparkled with astonishment. It was then faxed to me from the higher side that she would now be OK. Louise then left, I thanked my guides and felt very pleased to have remedied a painful and restrictive condition. Her long journey was not wasted.

Two days after Louise had consulted me with her shoulder problem I decided to sort out some monies which I wished to send by cheque to various animal welfare organisations. I finalised my choices and caught a bus to the town centre. It was nearing mid-day when I came out of a building society with a number of cheques to be posted off, still immersed in thought about certain charities that I had omitted from my list, I began to cross the one-way street directly outside, which was very narrow,.

Suddenly I was tugged, very firmly, backwards by my overcoat hood, nearly falling over in the process. I looked for the person responsible but realised that I was alone. As I composed myself, I quickly observed that a bus was thundering past at speed, the driver visibly shocked. His face looked drained. Brother Paul spoke to me, "My friend, we made arrangements to be at your side at this time to prevent you from being killed, for earlier today we knew about the sequence of events that would lead up to this possible tragedy and, being aware of free will, your absent-mindedness and your concentration on material matters, walking into the path of that bus was inevitable. Hence I pulled you way from danger. We do not want you over here just yet!" I was still in shock, apologised to my guides and promised to be more alert in future, although I knew I would in all probability fall back into my old absent-minded habits.

A week later the driver of the bus, whose face I had recognised during my close shave, approached Janet, as he had some time earlier lived in our street. He said, "I must confess Janet that to this day I cannot understand how I did not kill your husband. One minute he was walking in front of my bus, the next instant he seemed to be propelled backwards and I missed him by inches. The whole incident was totally unbelievable!" He added, " I admit I was travelling quite fast and had no time to stop. The thought of him going under my wheels gave me an almighty shock!" This episode further confirmed that our guardian spirits do intervene powerfully to prevent our transition from the earth plane if it does not suit God's wishes.

February 1995 had now shown its teeth; the first four days brought strong storms and snow. It was very cold and I chose to put on a thermal vest because my circulatory system had always caused me problems. On the third day of this month Christine Oakes, a neighbour and close friend of Janet, made a visit for a chat. Unfortunately Janet had popped out to her cousin's house. As Christine was a staunch Roman Catholic, we often had conversations about the implications of life after death.

During this particular debate I stressed that it was not possible for a priest to absolve a person's sins from week to week by hearing their confession and deciding upon the

114

appropriate penance, explaining that the soul carries all its life transgressions within the vibrations of its spirit and always judges itself when transition from the earth plane following death of the physical body takes place. Christine, for obvious reasons, spoke quite firmly stating that she could not accept my reasoning. Before she finished her sentence I was asked by Red Feathers to look into the kitchen.

I then saw a bright spirit outline near the work top, which was, Brother Paul. The breadcrock lid, which weighed about two kilos, was hovering precariously above the base of the container. Suddenly, the lid dropped back onto the breadcrock rim with a loud bang and for good measure was also twisted around twice, quite noisily. I looked at Christine who promptly jumped off the settee, her eyes widening considerably. She shrieked "What the hell was that Kevin?" I explained that it was my guides mischievous way of confirming that the point I had made earlier, doubting the validity of weekly confessions was accurate. She quickly donned her jacket, still visibly shocked and left the house, leaving a request for Janet to contact her later. Christine and I have had no further discussion on these religious points since, for a healthy respect by Chris for my viewpoint on the absolution of sin has now, thankfully, prevailed.

A week later the gas fires in the house were switched onto full heat as the temperature had dropped quite noticeably. Christine Garner of Sankey, Warrington contacted me via Frank Hutson, asking for assistance with her neck problem. Christine had worn a surgical collar continually for the previous two years, suffering from a slipped vertebrae, spondylosis and osteo-arthritis, she was in constant pain. I asked her to visit a few days later.

She arrived with a friend as she was a trifle apprehensive of psychic healing and needed a little support, Her friend sat quietly in the corner of the room. Christine settled on my favourite wooden chair. Information from the higher side was quickly conveyed. Psychic surgery was to be carried out, Mrs Garner's neck condition would be corrected through my fingers. I applied my hands for approximately five minutes and then checked her neck for mobility. She could now move it freely. Her friend had been watching the proceedings keenly throughout the healing. To make sure, I asked Christine to move her neck again, which she did freely.

Christine asked how much she owed me, I reminded her that there was no fee involved but she could help out with a donation to the local cats' protection league. My cat Susie seemed to nod her head in agreement as she lay on the sideboard watching the proceedings. The two ladies left the house, Christine with her neck collar now tucked under her arm. I thanked my guides and realised that my healing duties had now taken on larger and more responsible proportions.

In the last week of February 1995, Terry Butler, the musician whom I had earlier helped with a serious neck injury, rang me and asked if I would see his friend, Alan Maples, a keen cyclist from Sandbach, Cheshire, who was very shortly due to have an operation for a cartilage injury. Apparently, he was desperate to avoid surgery, although his specialist was adamant that to regain satisfactory mobility, surgery was essential.

He came down to my house three days later and on examination, his left leg was completely locked. Wan Chan informed me that his cartilage would be adjusted back into place by Red Feathers and that surgery would not be necessary. I placed his leg on a stool and pressed my thumb against his knee, the heat became quite intense and I felt a slight click. Alan then stood up and bent his leg. Full mobility had been restored, the cartilage had been re-adjusted back into its proper position. We were both extremely satisfied. Alan cancelled his operation and, to my knowledge, his knee has not troubled him since.

CHAPTER ELEVEN

February was proving very wet and damp. On the last day of the month, Mrs Nancy Armstrong of Redland Road, Bristol, rang me requesting help for her spinal problems. As I was providing healing at the time, I asked her to write to me setting out her requirements. Two days later I received her letter.

' She was quite elderly, in her eighties and had, fifteen years earlier, been involved in a serious car crash which resulted in her breaking nearly every bone in her body, necessitating two and a half years in hospital. She was now badly crippled, still suffering three crushed vertebrae and constantly in pain. Medical prognosis had given her no chance of relief or improvement. Whilst writing back to Mrs Armstrong, my guides informed me that permission had been granted on the higher side for a powerful intercession to be implemented.

A week later Mrs Armstrong rang to inform me that within hours of receiving my letter she had undergone a very strong inexplicable spiritual experience of detachment and indescribable physical sensations, which had lasted a full half hour. When this subsided she found, remarkably, that she had been cured of her disablement and pain and had finally discarded her crutches and steel corset.

My guides then informed me that they had attended to Mrs Armstrong shortly after her receiving my letter, removing all the fibrous adhesions that had formed on her damaged spinal discs and adjusting the facet joints of the various vertebrae which were all found to be incongruous. Wan Chan further told me that I would be instrumental in further intercessions when psychic surgery would be performed. I felt both humble and elated to be part of these new and important psychic developments.

March was steadily approaching and I was pleased to be seeing the back of winter. Steve Cowell, a friend came over to see me whilst I was having a drink in my local Pub. His wife Linda and her friend were quite frightened following simultaneous spiritual disturbances in their houses, both located in Stockton Heath, Warrington.

Linda's friend Jean McKeown had lost her husband, Brian, through a sudden heart attack two years earlier and since his death a succession of unnerving spiritual disturbances had taken place. Brian had materialised frequently in the presence of both Linda and Jean. Unfortunately, he had not accepted his death and was earthbound. As a result his haunting had attracted a restless, nasty spirit entity from the astral plane who delighted in plaguing Linda at her home, touching her indecently whilst she was sleeping and waking her with obscene chatter.

I arranged to go down a week later, prepared as required beforehand, and arrived at Linda's house first. I located the inferior spirit who was responsible for haunting her and dealt with him as necessary. I saw him quite literally rocketing towards his rightful spiritual dimension. A full blessing was administered to the house. I then made my way quickly to Jean's house.

On entering, I encountered a very cold atmosphere. Almost immediately her late husband Brian materialised in front of me, a confused expression on his face. I reminded him that he had died a physical death and now it was time for him to allow his wife to carry on with her earth life peacefully, stressing that they would be reunited in the spirit world some time in the future. Brother Paul had been at my side providing me with much inspiration and the necessary psychic power for the implementation of the soul rescue, his colours very bright as usual. I then carried out the procedures required for Brian's soul transition. The atmosphere soon began to warm up once again.

Jean was now much relieved following her husband's release from his earthbound state and Linda could sleep in peace with her spirit tormentor safely removed to his rightful spirit plane. I made my way home and felt that God's will had prevailed, once again tranquillity had been restored to both parties.

March 17th, St Patrick's day had arrived. I made my annual trip to the rear garden to take a small cutting of wood sorrel which closely resembles shamrock, to plant in the wooden stand situated in the front room. As I planted the cutting, the memory of Stephen Mason of Blackburn, Lancashire quickly resurfaced as he had made the stand for Janet and I before he sadly died of cancer six years earlier. His father, Gil Mason, had initially contacted me during the later stages of Stephen's illness asking for my healing services in the hope that I could possibly arrest the cancer or, better still, effect a cure.

Before Stephen arrived with his father my guides impressed upon me that my duties were to remove the fear of dying from Stephen and to educate him slowly about the realities of the earth life and the soul's subsequent passage to the spirit world. I had received no assurances from the higher side that my healing efforts would cure his condition.

I treated Stephen with spiritual healing on four occasions and actually improved his physical well-being. Each time I took the opportunity to fully explain to him about the mental, spirit and soul bodies, the various spirit realms and the law of karma, with its perfect operational patterns and the reason why so many seemingly innocent souls suffer through their earth lives with adversity and illness and why spiritual healing is not always successful with terminal illness.

Shortly after his final visit, his father Gil rang me with the sad news of Stephen's passing, albeit peacefully, in his local hospice. Most importantly, he was in his final moments totally prepared for death, having no fear at all. Gil thanked me for this assistance. I was disappointed somewhat as I felt that my efforts could have had a more positive outcome but then remembered that my role at this time was to ease Stephen's transition in the best possible manner.

I was to be brought in to carry out a similar function four years later when Michelle Johansson, a young local girl suffering from liver cancer, asked for my help. Once again this kind soul eventually passed to the higher side of life completely unafraid of dying after I had provided spiritual counselling over her final months of physical existence.

These experiences further developed my understanding of the different aspects of healing assistance which are necessary for fellow souls suffering from terminal illness. When a cure is not arranged through the higher side, counselling in spiritual laws is always crucially important in preparing the individual for the transition from physical death to the spiritual realms.

The days were becoming much lighter. Thankfully, April was just around the corner. Janet had invited a few of her friends to the house and I decided to pop down to the Ring O'Bells for a few pints. After settling down on a suitably hard bar stool in a quiet rear room and whilst carefully checking out my weekly rugby league handicap coupon, to my surprise Jean Robinson drifted into the room with a friend. She spotted me immediately and remarked in her usual 'chirpy' fashion, "Hello Kevin, we have just been to see a nationally known medium demonstrating at St Helens and stopped off here so that I could go to the ladies, I am quite desperate. The queue for the ladies at the theatre was endless!"

For some time I had been aware of an earthbound spirit male spirit presence in the Pub and accordingly have intimated to successive managers that sooner or later I would have to effect his transition. At this juncture circumstances dictated that it would not be too long before Jean would also be made aware, in a most embarrassing manner, of his presence. A few minutes passed then she hurried out of the ladies back to our table with a most startled expression on her face commenting anxiously, "Kevin you could have told me that this place is haunted. After using the toilet and whilst adjusting my clothes, a scruffy male spirit suddenly materialised, giggled and actually flushed the lavatory. What a bloody cheek!"

I assured Jean that I was fully aware of this character who was also not averse to regularly writing obscene remarks on the daily menu boards directed predominantly towards the female staff of the establishment. The staff had been unnerved for some time. My guides had informed me that this earthbound spirit was named Edward Tyler, a former tannery worker who died in the early part of this century. They added that he had always been lewd in character towards women young and old during his lifetime. I knew that his removal would be one of my next tasks and that his time to be exorcised was drawing closer.

On the Tuesday morning, of the second week in May, Janet had finally decided on her window box layout for the rear garden. I duly volunteered to purchase the necessary fertilizer and set off to the nearby DIY shop.

On returning home the phone rang. The caller was a Mrs Joyce Robertson, who lived in the Wilderspool Causeway area which is situated on the outskirts of Warrington. "Good morning, Mr McGrath - Mrs Robinson a medium who you know well has forwarded your number to me following my approach to her for help. She did not feel confident that she could resolve my problem. Therefore could you please help me?" "I will be pleased to intercede for you," I replied. She continued, "I have had a ghost problem since I moved into this property at the end of last year and the situation is getting worse." I paused for a few seconds during which time my guides assured me that they would assist me to remedy the haunting problem. I arranged to visit her on the following Monday afternoon which allowed me to carry out my customary psychic preparation at the weekend. I knew that an exorcism would be necessary.

Monday arrived and Joyce Robertson collected me from my home. During the journey she informed me of the phenomena which had been taking place, including continual power failures, hammering noises and obnoxious odours permeating throughout her dwelling. Most frightening of all, a large, dark shape intermittently followed her around the house at will and was regularly affecting her sleep patterns.

We arrived at the dwelling on Causeway Avenue and I investigated the ground floor finding a great deal of residual psychic energy. It was then impressed upon me by Brother Paul to head for the rear bedroom. I asked Joyce to stay on the ground floor and made my way upstairs.

On entering the bedroom, the atmosphere was chillingly cold. A large, ugly, dark male figure quickly materialised, levitated and hurtled rapidly towards me, obviously intent on attacking my aura. I ordered him to stop immediately, invoking the Christ force, which repelled him and also seemed to have the effect of shrinking him in size! I quickly completed the exorcism, the discarnate evil spirit was removed as required. Brother Paul then spoke quietly, "The inferior spirit had been in this house for many years, attracted by the psychic energy of a very depressed tenant. It has given me much pleasure watching you deal with his transition without our intervention." The room was now pleasantly warm again and the atmosphere much more friendly.

I descended the stairs slowly, reassured Mrs Robinson that the haunting problem had now been remedied properly and privately made my thanks to the God Head and his servants in spirit. Joyce was extremely relieved. On reaching home I completed the feeding of the window troughs before Janet arrived home from work, confident that the end result would be a riot of colours during the summer months which would lift our spirits immensely. It is a fact that flowers of all descriptions always replenish my psychic energies.

Mrs Phillippa Fauepel, a pleasant eighty one year old lady from Woolton, Liverpool, contacted me by phone at the beginning of June. I was rather concerned for her as she sounded most distressed and was obviously suffering much pain. Facts then emerged that for a period of seven weeks she had been experiencing excruciating pain in her stomach and lower abdomen. Conventional medicine had proved completely ineffective. Her anxiety and depression was not too surprising in the circumstances. She had obtained my details from a feature in the Psychic News.

She proceeded, "Mr McGrath, I am sure that I have been guided to contact you, please stop my pain." "Thank you for your trust and faith in me. I will ask my guides to attend to your condition and may you receive the treatment that I request," I replied. The telephone receiver was replaced and I proceeded to meditate, asking for a full spiritual intercession for Mrs Fauepel.

Almost immediately Red Feathers spoke to me kindly but quite firmly, "We will carry out spirit surgery to return the elderly lady to full health. She has suffered enough."

The following day soon after lunch, as I was compiling my absent healing list, the familiar tones of Doctor Chan penetrated my left ear, "Through your intercession of prayer we have used you as our medium and Mrs Fauepel has now been attended to successfully. Red Feathers and I have visited her, removed all the harmful bacteria and toxins from her stomach and colon. We have also cleared a partial blockage of the duodenum which was causing much pain and finally quietened her disturbed emotional state with an infusion of the divine healing source to ensure her convalescence. Her depressed state of mind will be lifted quickly." I thanked them for their spiritual intercession and continued to compile my healing list.

A week later Phillippa contacted me again to thank me for her recovery, confirming her well-being. Excitedly she described an extraordinary spiritual experience which had occurred soon after our initial contact. She explained that she had felt two arms gently lifting her to the sink. There followed a bout of induced vomiting although she had not previously experienced any feeling of nausea. Her pain ceased immediately. She continued to explain that for a period of twenty four hours her whole being was enveloped by a total state of calmness and serenity. I thanked her for the feedback, not letting her know that I had already been informed of this wonderful intercession by my guides. Nonetheless, I felt privileged to have been instrumental in lifting her pain and restoring peace and tranquillity to her mind and spirit.

CHAPTER TWELVE

The summer of 1995 was truly glorious. The sun was a very warm friend and allowed me to restore vital energies which had been depleted over the previous year, but it was a date later that year Tuesday, 10th October, to be precise, which was to prove particularly memorable for two reasons.

The first involved a close escape from serious injury after slipping carelessly on a telephone directory at the top of the staircase early one morning. Luckily for me my 'neat dive' down the stairs was interrupted by the balustrade and left me bruised, shaken and in pain but nonetheless relieved that the damage had not been more severe.

The second reason for recalling this day concerns the successful healing of Mrs Denise Roeborough of Newton Aycliffe, County Durham. She had contacted me because she had been suffering from considerable spinal pain for eight years due to a disc problem. Her orthopaedic specialist had ruled out surgical intervention and all the therapeutic treatments she had received had failed to ease the pain with the result that she had to take a narcotic-based drug every day. She had made contact the previous week and a visit was arranged for one afternoon.

The journey over had taken the best part of four hours and had proved most uncomfortable because of her condition. I had insisted on contact healing as my guides had indicated that they wished me to attend to her in this way. When Denise arrived she hobbled very slowly into the house with the aid of two walking sticks. She was clearly in excruciating pain and had lost the proper use of both legs. The healing was swift - her discs were heard to click back in place and I assured her that the spiritual healing which had been applied would be successful within a very short time.

The following day she phoned me up out of sheer relief to tell me excitedly that all the pain had disappeared and her movements were no longer restricted. She was most appreciative and somewhat moved by the experience. Her general practitioner, who was also informed of her recovery, kindly accepted that an inexplicable cure had taken place and admitted that he firmly believed in spiritual healing as a complementary therapy.

Later that day I asked for a little extra help from my guides for myself - to reduce the bruising and persistent aching in my joints following the tumble on the staircase but the request fell on deaf ears and I remained very sore for days. The lesson had to be learned.

On the eighteenth of October, Mrs Barbara Falconer of Netherburn, Larkhill, Lanarkshire contacted me with a request for distant healing for her husband James who was seriously ill in hospital with acute heart problems. The hospital staff were of the opinion that his life was in the balance. I asked my guides to attend to him and they conveyed to me that permission had been granted from the higher side for spiritual surgery to be carried out.

Twenty four hours later Barbara informed me from the hospital that James had miraculously recovered. The surgeon admitted that the heart had undergone mystifying structural changes restoring Mr Falconer's heart function to a normal pattern. To the present day James Falconer is energetic, strong and well thanks to the radiant spirit doctors from the higher side.

It is always helpful and heart warming when fellow souls who have received the benefits of my healing provide me with feedback and also kindly share their experiences through the channels of the media. Press coverage etc., in particular, enables me to help more people in need.

The following letters are a few typical examples:

Mrs Dorothy Shakeshaft of Holly Avenue,
Bradwell, Gt. Yarmouth.

19-9-95

Dear Mr Kevin McGrath,

I saw the orthopaedic Doctor after having the plaster taken off my arm and he said it looked good, but I would need some physiotherapy on my wrist and fingers. I asked if I could have it done at my own doctor's surgery and was told it would be alright, but I wasn't able to see her until the 6th September as she was on holiday.

When she did see it she kept saying "I can't believe it," that it was "absolutely remarkable" and that it didn't seem possible that a broken wrist (of about six weeks) should be so near normal, and said I didn't need any physiotherapy and she couldn't understand why I haven't had any pain or aching with it. I feel sure it must be due to all the help you and your spirit helpers have given me. I am very grateful. I have to see the hospital doctor again on the 28th September.

I am also pleased to say that my right leg is feeling much better too, the aching in my hip has almost gone, and the pain in my right knee has almost gone too. Many, many thanks.

Mr Derek Barber of East Green, Southwold, Suffolk.
Letter to Psychic News, November 1995.

Dear Editor,

I also acted on a Psychic News article earlier this year regarding Warrington healer Kevin McGrath, who agreed to give me absent healing. For over 30 years I have endured back and leg problems, never without pain of varying degrees. I did not tell Kevin the root of the problem nor the particular vertebrae concerned, yet he was able to confirm that problem and the precise vertebrae.

Since receiving absent healing my back and leg pain has greatly decreased. On the really good days I can now move about at something like my old speed and virtually free of pain. For many *years I was quite unable to sleep on my left side at all due to the extreme discomfort: I can do so now with complete ease and rest.*

Only those who have to live day after day with pain know how debilitating it is, but the quality of my life has distinctly improved - thanks to Kevin and his guides.

Mrs Esther Robinson of Union Road, London SW8.

31st August 1995

Dear Mr McGrath

Sometime last March I wrote to you to request spiritual healing for my husband and myself. With regard to myself, the Doctor's said that there is nothing to worry about ... and I believed that your help has done wonders. The healing that my husband received was brilliant. I cannot express my gratitude to you and to your Spirit Guide for the great help you have sent us ... Words cannot express how grateful I am that my husband's leg was saved.

Mrs Patricia Castle of Brookland Road,
Huish Episcopi, Longport, Somerset.

31-01-96

Dear Mr McGrath,

Where do I start? First of all, thank you so much for taking my phone call on Saturday last, you made it so easy to talk.

On Sunday night, Monday morning when I went to bed, I made myself comfortable, and a thought kept going through my head to 'lay straight'. I ignored it for a while, thinking to myself - 'I'm comfortable as I am' but the thought was still there - eventually making me take the decision to 'lay straight' at 0115 hours.

I was still awake when I experienced my legs - only my legs - jumping down the bed - nothing else. I remember thinking whatever made my legs jump like that? Before I've jumped when going off to sleep but this felt different. I remember looking at the time but didn't connect it at this stage with our chat. I then slept wonderfully well, which I never do at night and my back pain always woke me on moving.

In the morning I got out of bed, halfway to the bathroom I realised I was standing up straight - from my bed usually I would be bending over and have to gradually straighten up, going through as I say a 'pain barrier' but no longer, I am walking and standing up straight.

Once in the bathroom whilst waking up, I began to put things together - no surely not - it can't be - not this quick ... Anyway whatever, to have lost the pain is just so wonderful. I think you know I am so grateful. Once again thank you and, as you say, the 'wonderful souls' that you work for, you must be very honoured to have been chosen ... God Bless ...

Mr Ernie Sears of Netley Albey, Hampshire.
Letter to Psychic News April 1996

Dear Madam:

Further to our phone conversation of a few minutes ago I thought I'd enlarge on the incidents related while they are fairly fresh in my memory! Since Christmas I have had an "inflamed" stomach. I have been a healer myself since it was all dropped into my lap in 1979 and know how "stress" and the "mind" can affect one physically, but even that didn't help in this case, the discomfort came and went. On Saturday the 3rd February this year ... I was in real trouble...twinges, that "inflamed" feeling etc. etc. Having given various people Kevin McGrath's name and address after reading good reports of this Cheshire healer in Psychic News, I thought, why don't I write for myself? I sat down that very afternoon and wrote the letter, sealed it ready for the Sunday post, settled down for an evening of television and general rest. I saw no television until much later!

I went out like the proverbial light on my lounge settee ... for one hour ... "came to" for a while, feeling very feverish and disorientated, then "off" I went again for another hour! I can recall "dreaming" about somewhere with "pipes" and "tubes" all around me ... weird!

*Finally woke up about 10.00pm, almost three hours had gone ...
feeling absolutely wonderful! No discomfort.*

*Having had an almost similar experience ... without the "dreams"
in 1983 when a terrible back problem "went" as I was writing to the
late Ted Fricker, a famous London healer ... that never came back
... but this time, I thought, the good feeling I had was only
temporary, the problem would come back the next day as it did
sometimes. But no! I felt twenty years younger than my 71 ... I am
a keen country and western fan and go dancing two or three times
a week ... almost destroyed my lady partners that weekend and the
ones that followed! "Exuberant" was the description!*

*Wrote to Kevin McGrath to describe the situation ... he had already
replied to my original cry for help ... and today, twelve days after
the related happenings, he rang me to explain that I'd been
"operated on" by those spirit doctors ... hence they had "put me out"
that Saturday evening while they attended a duodenal ulcer that
would have been serious had it continued its growth. I could accept
that!*

*I could only describe the cessation of the discomfort as like someone
pushing a button and turning me off!*

*I fully understand that "mind" and "pure thought" can work
miracles ... when writing for help my "mind" was tuned in to the
vibrational plane where the healing hails from. No way could I
"heal" myself ... if readers have tried that they'll know it isn't easy!*

*Needless to say I have told others of my acquaintance of Kevin
McGrath... and suggest they contact him. After all, if you don't
ask, you don't get! I have found, too, that the experience has
deepened my awareness of the world that lies often unseen, around
us.*

CHAPTER THIRTEEN

Saturday the 11th November provided a little light relief from two incidents. The first was an encounter with a local 'Born-again' Christian group who regularly preached to the masses in Warrington town centre.

During the morning, as I was on my way to the main post office, I happened to walk past their leader, whose interpretation of the scriptures was noisy to say the least. He quickly levelled his threats of eternal damnation towards me as he obviously regarded those who are psychically oriented as modern day 'wizards' and in the service of 'Satan' himself.

This tirade, delivered with a smile, did not upset me. My riposte was swift as I carefully pointed out several glaring contradictions in the Old Testament and asked him for an explanation. My request had the most welcome effect of ensuring a few minutes of silence for the passing shoppers, as no answer was forthcoming. I continued on my way, quietly satisfied.

Later that afternoon back at home a spirit child paid a visit and provided the second amusing episode. John and Rose McSweeney had travelled from Scotland to stay with one of Janet's friends. We had met them briefly twelve months earlier at a wedding anniversary party and they had decided to pop down and see us before taking the train back to Glasgow.

Minutes before their arrival I was measuring the bathroom window before I ordered new curtains. I was aware of the presence of a spirit child named 'Peter' who had visited me several times before and seemed to enjoy my company. I never attempted to rescue him as my guides informed me that his visits were carefully arranged by the higher side to broaden his earth experience which had tragically been cut short by illness in the post war period. He materialised, moved close to my side smiling broadly and promptly faded.

As I walked back downstairs John stepped out of the living room and quipped, "Kevin, your wee bairn soon disappeared upstairs when we came in. Is he shy?" Janet had been busy making tea and sandwiches and looked understandably puzzled. I replied in a guarded fashion, "We have a family of moggies but no children, unfortunately!" John and Rose appeared shocked. John gathered himself and remarked, "Well, who the hell was the curly-headed boy running up the stairs?" They listened as I explained that he was, in fact, a ghost but I knew instinctively that they could not accept what they had so clearly seen. After tea they quaffed two large whiskies and left for the station still visibly shaken.

On November 13th, Mr Terence Cholmondeley, a social worker living in Warrington, phoned me following press coverage of an exorcism which I had carried out some weeks earlier. His tone was firm but anxious and the reasons for his approach soon became clear as he explained that his disabled mother Mrs Edna Cholmondeley, a seventy five year old widow, had been subjected to an inexplicable series of vile sexual assaults by an unseen presence. These had been taking place at frequent intervals over a period of six months and she had become extremely distressed by what was happening.

She lived alone in the Clock Face district of St Helen's Merseyside and I was told that she was in urgent need of my spiritual help. The attacks always took place during the night when she was sleeping and finally, in desperation, she had sought refuge in the kitchen in an attempt to escape the nightly hell.

My instincts told me that the incidents Terence related to me were thoroughly genuine and that the spirit responsible for these ungodly acts was of a very low and perverted nature. I decided that my intervention was indeed necessary and should be initiated as soon as possible.

On the following day I made my usual psychic preparation for strength and protection and travelled with Terence to his mother's bungalow in Gersey Lane. As we entered I felt an overpowering presence of evil permeating the place. Mrs

Cholmondeley was a charming lady and greeted us with a brave smile as she reclined in her armchair at the side of the fire.

I had to cut short our opening conversation as a huge, dark male spirit shape suddenly materialised beside her chair. His face was extremely ugly reflecting his nature and he bore a marked resemblance to a gargoyle and although his clothing was ragged I realised that it was from the Edwardian period. In a deliberate attempt to taunt me, he lifted up Mrs Cholmondeley's skirt - a lewd action which filled me with disgust and left Edna and Terence badly shaken. I knew that he had to be exorcised immediately to ensure her future well-being as she would otherwise surely be tormented further by this inferior spirit until her life force was totally depleted.

An exorcism was rapidly conducted despite the fact that the entity, once realising my intention to remove him, made several unsuccessful attempts to attack me and breach my aura. My guides were obviously aware of this development as in a matter of seconds he was enveloped in a shaft of radiant light and then propelled through the astral doorway with great force. His prolonged stay on the earth plane had finally been terminated.

Afterwards I informed Edna and Terence that a spirit clearance had been effected and reassured them that peace and normality would now be quickly restored to the house. I felt much satisfaction and relief that God's will had prevailed. Three weeks later I received a call from Terence who was happy to be able to confirm that there had been no more attacks since the day of the exorcism and that his dear mother had regained peace of mind once more.

Some days later as I checked my post two letters caught my attention. One was from Marian Williams, a young lady from Bangor and carried good news. She had been suffering from severe rheumatoid arthritis and had travelled up to visit me for healing during the early part of 1995 but she now wrote that following the healing the condition had eased continually and her mobility had improved by fifty percent and she had also experienced a great reduction in the pain. I thanked my guides once again for their strong and compassionate intercession.

In the second letter Mr Barber of Widnes spoke of a serious case of spirit disturbance. Reading between the lines I sensed menace and torment.

I contacted Mr Barber later that evening and reassured him that I would help his daughter and try my very best to resolve the long-standing haunting problems which were causing so much anxiety and distress. A time was arranged for me to be picked up five days later on the outskirts of the town to avoid heavy daytime traffic.

Mr Barber collected me as arranged on the 20th November and as we travelled I told him that the troublesome spirit responsible for so many years of disruption would probably be aware of my proposed intervention in view of an earlier reaction outlined in the letter. Moreover, I expected to meet powerful resistance to the exorcism.

Thirty minutes later we arrived at the semi-detached house where Mrs Carr and her thirteen year old autistic son met us at the rear entrance. Both appeared drained and very edgy. I introduced myself briefly, blessed the ground floor rooms and then made my way upstairs to the front bedroom where I felt sure that the troublesome spirit was located.

Before I reached the landing a powerful field of energy suddenly forced me back down the staircase, so I gathered myself together and prayed slowly invoking the Christ-force, and the energy field was quickly dissipated. I now moved to the bedroom to engage the spirit. As I entered a small, hostile, elderly-looking male spirit rapidly materialised. Our eyes met and our wills locked. He expressed his intention to remain in his earthbound state and his determination to continue to torment Lorraine and Martin.

It was conveyed to me by Brother Paul that the discarnate spirit had regularly been utilising psychic energy from Martin's aura and this explained all the psychic phenomena that had taken place over the past eight years. My intention to forcibly remove him was quickly relayed. The exorcism was carried out with a great deal of power and I felt somewhat relieved as he was escorted away by the bright ones in spirit.

I returned to the living room and with much pleasure informed the family that their living nightmare was over at last, giving them a short explanation of the exorcism procedure. I left for home, task accomplished. As a matter of courtesy I checked the situation with Lorraine two months later and she told me that the haunting had finally ceased. God's will had prevailed - I knew that the difficult spirit was well and truly placed in his rightful spiritual realm.

When I reflected on the evil nature and the force of the spirit I had encountered it had been one of the strongest I had ever faced during all my years of spirit clearance.

A week later as Janet settled down eagerly to watch another episode of Coronation Street and I was resting my back on the front room floor we heard someone knocking loudly on the front door. When I opened it John Finnigan, a tall man in his early twenties presented himself. He seemed extremely agitated and blurted out a disturbing account of several paranormal incidents at his house in North Avenue, Warrington which had badly affected his partner and frightened their three young children.

He insisted that Carol had been raped repeatedly by a foul smelling spirit and that the children had been systematically pushed to the floor while both he and Carol were present. They had already approached a catholic priest for help but he refused to visit the house. He did, however provide them with his personal crucifix but this had failed to stem the wave of psychic attacks.

John also told me that he had been woken up in the early hours of the morning by a loud, eerie howling noise and had seen a ghostly figure leaning on Carol as she lay sleeping. On getting dressed the following morning he was surprised to find several scratch marks on his face and arms. The intuitive alarm bells in my head rang in a familiar way and I knew that John and his family needed help immediately. He was clearly relieved when I agreed to investigate.

Two days later, following two hours of preparation, I visited the house which was in the middle of a council estate near to the town centre. On investigation I located two depraved spirit individuals of a very low vibration who had been earthbound for hundreds of years. Both appeared dishevelled, reeked of alcohol and were wearing sailor's uniforms from the early part of the nineteenth century. They were extremely hostile and moved rapidly towards me gesticulating furiously and showing anger on their faces. They were obviously determined to intimidate me and tried to knock me off balance but were repulsed equally quickly. Thereupon a very strong exorcism and thorough house blessing was carried out.

John contacted me three weeks later but this time his voice sounded far more confident and he seemed to be in good spirits. The haunting had stopped. I knew that the family finally had peace and that their terrible ordeal was over.

The Christmas period came and went with unbelievable speed but it did allow Janet and I to relax somewhat and to entertain friends and relatives. It was also a sad time as two of my favourite stray tom cats had disappeared. My instincts told me they had been 'cat-napped' by some cruel souls for their beautiful coats. I had to console myself with the knowledge that we would be reunited at some time in the distant future in the spirit world.

CHAPTER FOURTEEN

Early in the new year we were in the icy grip of winter so I wrapped up well in an ex-army issue woollen pullover and a thick pair of corduroy trousers and travelled to a local catholic church to obtain a fresh supply of holy water. My guides had forewarned me that my spiritual services would be required quite soon and for a variety of purposes.

When I arrived I found that for the umpteenth time the church was locked and I had to request access at the priest's residence. The housekeeper there was not very helpful and I could sense quite clearly that she thought I was a shady character. It was only after producing my first communion medal that I managed to persuade her to allow me to get the water I needed. I decided that in future I would have a shave and dress more formally to avoid repeating this experience.

Roger McGuiness, a retired docker from Bootle, Liverpool was suffering from a long-standing back complaint and he visited me a week later after his wife Gwen had made the arrangements by letter. When he arrived he hobbled into my house, his face wracked with pain. I certainly knew how he felt as my lower spine was also causing me considerable discomfort. As the healing was applied, I felt and saw the strength of the rays directed to his body and his phone call the following day to inform me of his cure was not unexpected. I felt very pleased that his suffering had stopped because only those who have to endure chronic back pain can be aware of its most debilitating effect on the body and mind.

A short time after seeing Roger, Millie Hudson, a local lady who had moved to Newton-Le-Willows, called at my house with her sister, Dorothy Matthews. Millie had received spiritual healing earlier for a troublesome condition and the results were so good that she persuaded Dorothy to visit me as one of her legs was numb, badly swollen and she was very concerned about this. X rays had not shown up any abnormalities and a course of antibiotics had failed to reduce the swelling.

Whilst she was there Dr Chan informed me that the problem was being caused by a blockage in an artery and would be remedied through the application of spiritual healing. Ten minutes later the healing treatment was finished and Dorothy was able to walk away from the house with her mobility restored. The swelling had also been greatly reduced and feeling in the limb was back to normal. I thanked Dr Chan and Red Feathers for their healing applications and settled down to a refreshing can of Murphy's stout.

I had been notified by my guides some time before that an exacting schedule of spirit clearance work was to come, and as fate would have it, an enforced week's bed rest, the result of severe muscle spasms in my back conveniently allowed me to strengthen my psychic energy reserves in anticipation. The expected period of activity began in mid-February and finished on 25th March. Two powerful exorcisms were conducted and two soul rescues were carried out, one of which was particularly memorable.

On Monday, 12 February a soul rescue took place at East Lane, Orford Estate, Warrington. A female apparition had regularly been seen by both Peter and Mary Murphy walking aimlessly through the ground floor rooms. This earthbound spirit was apparently oblivious to their presence. I identified the spirit as Mrs James, a previous tenant who had died eight years earlier. She had a bemused look on her face as if she had lost her way somehow, and was totally unaware of anything around her. She was 'schoolmarmish' in appearance, being very primly dressed; she wore her hair in a bun and in fact reminded of one of my old primary school teachers. This was a quiet but successful soul rescue with her loved ones in spirit in attendance to help guide her slowly through the astral gateway towards her rightful home in the spirit realms.

On Wednesday, 21st February I undertook an exorcism at Rosemary Avenue, Stockton Heath, Warrington for Sue Craft. Sue had been subjected to nightly assaults by a male spirit. These involved sexual molestation and alarming attempts to strangle her. Her fourteen year old son was also being tormented by voices and knocking noises while he slept.

On investigation the perpetrator was quickly located and turned out to be a balding, male spirit form wearing a demob suit with a white scarf wound around his neck, typical of that post war era. He had very small, cold, piercing blue eyes and I had the distinct impression that other evil forces were ready to come to his aid. However, after a prolonged struggle, the negative forces were dispelled by Brother Paul and the malevolent entity was observed disappearing through a tunnel of light, his earthbound residence happily brought to an end. Two weeks later Sue's husband Harry contacted me to confirm that the haunting problem had been resolved.

On Tuesday, March 5th I effected another exorcism at Lilac Grove, Stockton Heath, Warrington where Wendy Tollet reported that she, too, was being attacked during her sleep. She was terrified because her spirit assailant had made several attempts to suffocate her and to add to her distress she could hear knocking sounds at regular intervals when there was no logical explanation.

I visited her house after lunch one day, located a discarnate presence and carried out a strong exorcism. On this occasion I did not encounter much resistance. The atmosphere when I entered was very heavy and cold and this had also been lifted, much to my pleasure. Confirmation of the clearance was given to me ten days later by her husband Simon.

Shortly before dealing with Sue's problem I had been approached by Joan Davis, a sprightly seventy year old widow who called at my house whilst I was out undergoing physiotherapy. Janet was at home and she recognised Mrs Davis instantly as she lived nearby in a terraced house which was situated next to an old farmhouse in Marsh House Lane. "Is Kevin in?" she asked nervously, "I must see him! Believe me, I cannot stay in that house one more night!" Janet informed Joan of my whereabouts and after listening to a brief outline of an obvious haunting problem which was making Joan's life a misery, reassured her that I would pop round to the house that evening.

When I reached the house later that evening and she invited me in the whole place was tingling and I noticed immediately the startling brightness of her aura which indicated great psychic sensitivity. I was very aware of a powerful spirit presence in the place, although it did not appear to be threatening or evil. Joan greeted me warmly, settled down on her settee and quickly told me of the regular visits of three girl spirit forms to her bedroom, all clad in Victorian dress.

For three consecutive nights they had woken her up in the early hours by banging on the bedroom door and opening and shutting it. Then they proceeded, mischievously, to prod and tease her until she was forced eventually to move downstairs into the living room. The game continued as she slept on the settee with one of the spirit children blowing on her face to further disturb her night's rest.

Joan was clairvoyant and so had seen all three spirit forms quite clearly, hence her reasons for wanting to move away from the house as soon as possible. I had taken the precaution earlier of protecting my aura although my instincts told me that I would not be attacked on this occasion. When I eventually confronted the children who were dressed in Victorian clothes it was almost as if they were pleading for final release, although not overtly. My guides informed me that they had lived in the proximity of the farmhouse and this was their old playground. They had died quite young - around the age of nine or ten, in the same year, just before the turn of the century. Two had contracted meningitis and the third little girl had developed septicaemia.

I walked up the staircase very slowly as I was still feeling the effects of the physiotherapist's heavy-handed manipulation. Then I went into the front bedroom where I knew that the spirit presence was at its most powerful and fixed my gaze on the end of the bed. Slowly, the three spirit children, all with colourful surrounding auras materialised. One pointed at me and the others chuckled loudly and begged me to join in their game with Mrs Davies. I, in turn, spoke to them as softly a possible conveying my intention to have them reunited with their loved ones in the spirit world. They seemed to understand their inevitable journey was near and smiled at me with great affection.

They passed on swiftly but to the end they expressed their wish to carry on playing within the realm of the 'earth playground'. The necessary prayers were said for a swift release of the divine source to ensure a full and proper release from their earthbound state. With great satisfaction I witnessed their individual guardian spirits leading them away up a glorious shaft of light to their parents awaiting them with outstretched hands.

Mrs Davis was informed of the 'soul rescue' that had taken place and I reassured her that life would soon return to normal. The whole experience was truly memorable for me because of the underlying eagerness with which the young spirits had demonstrated for help in their release, which fortunately I had been able to facilitate, despite their early reluctance to cooperate.

Following the period of strong spirit clearance work which I had been carrying out, I welcomed the opportunity to be of service in another very important capacity which was to provide fellow souls with evidence of survival of their loved ones from physical death. To this end Louise Middleton of Padgate, Warrington visited me in late March. She had been directed to me by David Buchan, a staff nurse whom I had met some years earlier. David asked me to help her out with what he considered to be a case of depression.

As she walked into my living room hesitantly four bright spirit figures, three adults and a very young child, quickly materialised at her side. One kind looking male of middle-aged appearance clairaudiently identified himself as Louise's father. He continued by informing me that he had recently passed over and was accompanied by his parents and nephew who had died soon after birth. The infant had continued to grow in the spirit world, he explained. Details of his occupation before death as a cabinet maker were also conveyed with an assurance that he was settled in the spirit world.

I looked at Louise who seemed deeply interested in my obvious concentration and told her of the message. She immediately became upset but later was happy to confirm that the information relating to her father and other deceased relatives was accurate in all respects. Louise left soon afterwards, thanking me for my time.

When I spoke to David a few days later it transpired that Louise had originally visited me to receive spiritual healing and that the depression she was experiencing was caused by the loss of her father. She had been lifted by his comforting message and the evidence of his survival had proved to be wonderful tonic for her.

Although most people on requesting spiritual healing were open and direct with their requirements, there was the odd occasion when they were less than honest about their needs. A typical example involved Beryl Hatton of Woodlands Drive, Thelwall, Cheshire. Early in April she travelled to see me following a request for help with blurred vision.

During the healing session my guides informed me that Beryl was also suffering from pain in her shoulder and arm with a partial loss of use in her hand. The problems were being caused by a bulging disc trapping a root nerve in her upper spine. I mentioned the condition to Beryl who admitted that she had been reluctant to seek help for the problem fearing that she would be labelled a hypochondriac as several X-rays over a period of two years had proved inconclusive. Knowing that both her eye and back problems were being addressed from the higher side, I was optimistic of an overall improvement.

Seven days later Beryl wrote to thank me with the news that her eye condition was steadily improving, but more importantly that her arm and shoulder pain had disappeared with the full use of her hand having been restored. Her long-standing discomfort was not psychosomatic in origin, an opinion which she was beginning to believe. In light of Beryl's experience, X-rays are obviously not totally effective in locating trapped nerves.

I had also received other pleasing news in a letter from Mrs Pramilia Hunte of Hindley Road, Harrow, Middlesex. Her uncle, Dr N Dhewar, who had been seriously ill in a Mexican hospital prior to Christmas had completely recovered. As his condition at the time had been causing much concern Mrs Hunte had telephoned to request my help with distant healing. Following my intercession Dr Dhewan rapidly regained full health and was discharged from hospital a week later. This healing success was further confirmation that distance was certainly no obstacle for my radiant spirit guides.

At the end of May, spring was giving way to my favourite season, summer. The long hours of daylight and warmer winds never failed to lift my spirits. However, the rambling honeysuckle in my rear garden looked very sad indeed with its stems and flowers smothered in aphids. I generally accepted that all God's creations had a right to live but blackfly I was prepared to exclude from my consideration. Insecticide spray was swiftly and heavily applied blitzing the bugs until the battle was won. My sweet-scented friend would undoubtedly, repay me in kind throughout the coming months.

With thoughts to the future a varied timetable of further spiritual involvement has, no doubt, been carefully orchestrated by those bright spirit guides to whom I have long been privileged to belong. I have prayed that I remain strong enough to carry out any further duties that are required of me, although it has been impressed upon me by my guides that vascular disease poses a great threat to my well-being and I should take soya lecithin, Ginkgo Biloba and root ginger daily to aid my circulation and also adjust my diet accordingly. However, God's will for the soul's transition always prevails and my mission continues ....

ADDENDUM

PROCEDURES FOR THE PRACTICE OF EXORCISM
AND SOUL RESCUE OPERATIONS

The under-mentioned procedures should preferably be undertaken by persons who have undergone a proper grounding in spiritual development and who are naturally psychically sensitive. This capability will also help the channelling of communications between the instrument chosen for the task, and the discarnate spirit/s, to be carried out more clearly and effectively.

EXORCISM

An exorcism is deemed necessary when a discarnate earthbound spirit is of a malevolent disposition and the cause of much distress to those souls in a physical body who he or she chooses to haunt and torment. This category of spirit is usually reluctant to move to their rightful spirit realm because there might be a very good chance that unpleasant conditions may be faced, owing to its lower vibrations and karmic responsibilities.

When it is time for the troublesome spirit's proper transition, force must be employed during the procedure as persuasion or cajolement will not usually be effective. A special time to carry out the exorcism is arranged with the persons requesting assistance. The following preparation should be used prior to departing to the dwelling or premises which is/are being haunted:-

a)   A visit to a church for prayer to the God-head and to immerse oneself within the Christ force.

b)   A brief period of meditation to be undertaken

c)   The wearing of a set of rosary beads and a crucifix beforehand, to be removed only after completion of the exorcism

d)   A container of holy water from the church should also be taken to the troubled location for blessing purposes

e)   Resist accommodating thoughts of any impure nature so as not to lower one's spiritual vibrations

f)   A protective prayer is to be used to safeguard your aura from possible attack by an inferior spirit or spirits or malevolent forces (this prayer is a

modification of the original composed by Dion Fortune, Publication -
Psychic Self Defence).

The prayer is as follows and should be spoken prior to leaving for your
destination to conduct the exorcism:-

"BY THE POWER OF THE CHRIST, OF GOD THE FATHER
WITHIN ME (MAKING THE SIGN OF THE CROSS
SIMULTANEOUSLY) WHOM I SERVE WITH ALL MY
HEART, WITH ALL MY SOUL AND WITH ALL MY
STRENGTH."

Whilst praying, extend your hands forward in front of you, touch to a point,
then sweep around to your back again, touching the fingertips together,
saying simultaneously

"I ENCOMPASS ABOUT MYSELF WITH THE DIVINE
CIRCLE OF HIS PROTECTION ACROSS WHICH NO
MORTAL ERROR DARES TO SET ITS FOOT, AMEN."

On arrival at the dwelling/premises, it is important to locate the troublesome
spirit/s and then clearly convey your intentions to forcibly remove
him/her/them to his/her/their rightful spirit realm. All rooms are then blessed
with holy water with the prayer

"IN THE NAME OF THE FATHER, THE SON AND THE
HOLY SPIRIT, AMEN."

The following procedure is then employed.

For the removal and disposal of any negative residual energies that may be
found on investigation, the first prayer is used:-

"BY THE SUPREME WILL AND POWER OF OUR
ALMIGHTY FATHER, I CLEANSE THIS/THESE
DWELLING/PREMISES OF ALL MALEVOLENT, IMPURE,
AND DESTRUCTIVE FORCES, AMEN."

For the forceful treatment from the earth plane of the malevolent, inferior spirit/s, the second prayer is used:-

"IN THE NAME AND POWER OF GOD ALMIGHTY AND THE HOLINESS AND SACRED NAME OF JESUS CHRIST OUR LORD AND SAVIOUR, I COMMAND YOU TO DEPART FROM THIS/THESE DWELLING/PREMISES AT ONCE AND GO TO YOUR RIGHTFUL PLACE AS PREPARED IN GOD'S SPIRIT REALMS, AMEN."

Then repeat prayer as above to intensify power of exorcism. The third prayer is one of thanks, to be used as follows:-

"DEAR HEAVENLY FATHER, I THANK YOU FOR THE ABUNDANT RELEASE OF YOUR DIVINE SOURCE WHICH HAS ENABLED ME THROUGH YOUR SERVANTS IN SPIRIT TO EFFECT THE PROPER TRANSITION OF THIS/THESE INFERIOR SPIRIT/S TO ITS/THEIR RIGHTFUL SPIRITUAL PLANE, AMEN."

SOUL RESCUE

The process of enabling a discarnate spirit who, by nature, is not malevolent, to be released from the earth plane is categorised as soul rescue.

Frequently, the earthbound individual, following release from physical life, is confused, refusing to accept the death that has occurred, sometimes tied to material surroundings, deeply worried about unfinished business on the earth, or tied to a loved one in the flesh who is suffering much grief over a lengthy period following their passing many earthbound souls are simply crying out for help to be released to their proper spirit dimension.

Contact is made with the spirit as mentioned before in the passage referring to the conduction of exorcism. Your intention is also conveyed that you are to effect their transition to the spirit realm which is best suited to their vibration reassurance is necessary that loved ones who have previously passed eagerly await their arrival.

FIRST PRAYER TO BE USED AS FOLLOWS
(singular or group earthbound spirit usage):-

"DEAR HEAVENLY FATHER, I CALL UPON YOUR DIVINE NAME AND ALMIGHTY POWER TO ENABLE YOUR DISCARNATE SERVANTS TO EFFECT THE PROPER TRANSITION OF THIS/THESE CONFUSED AND LOST SPIRIT/S TO ITS/THEIR RIGHTFUL PLACE IN YOUR HEAVENLY REALMS, AMEN."

SECOND PRAYER TO BE USED AS FOLLOWS:-

"O RESTLESS AND CONFUSED SOUL/S, I FIRMLY REQUEST IN THE POWER OF OUR ALMIGHTY FATHER, AND IN THE HOLY NAME OF OUR LORD JESUS CHRIST AND THROUGH THE HOLY SPIRIT, THAT YOU FOLLOW THE DIVINE LIGHT AND DEPART FROM THIS/THESE DWELLING/PREMISES ONCE AND FOR ALL, TO YOUR RIGHTFUL PLACE IN THE SPIRIT REALMS WHERE YOUR LOVED ONES AWAIT YOU AMEN."

All rooms are then blessed with holy water as previously mentioned in the passage on exorcism. The second prayer of thanks is used as mentioned before, in conduction of the exorcism.

Full preparation as carried out before the conduction of an exorcism should also be completed to ensure full and proper protection during the soul rescue ceremony from intruding inferior spirits.